NON-FICTION.

362.764 S698w

Sonkin, Daniel Jay
Wounded boys, heroic men :a man's g
uide to recovering from child abuse

DISCARDED BY
MEAD PUBLIC LIBRARY

W9-BPO-125

4/99

Wounded
Boys
Heroic
Men

DISCARD
MEAD P.L.

Wounded Boys Heroic Men

A Man's Guide to Recovering from Child Abuse

Daniel Jay Sonkin, Ph.D.

Adams Media Corporation
HOLBROOK, MASSACHUSETTS

To Marissa Teal. . . . with all my love

Copyright ©1998, by Daniel Jay Sonkin, Ph.D. All rights reserved.
This book, or parts thereof, may not be reproduced in any form
without permission from the publisher; exceptions are made for
brief excerpts used in published reviews.

Published by Adams Media Corporation
260 Center Street, Holbrook, MA 02343

ISBN: 1-58062-010-8

Printed in the United States of America.

J I H G F E D C B A

Library of Congress Cataloging-in-Publication Data
Sonkin, Daniel Jay.
Wounded boys, heroic men : a man's guide to recovering from child abuse /
by Daniel Jay Sonkin.
p.   cm.
Originally published: Stamford, CT : Longmeadow Press, 1992.
Includes bibliographical references and index.
ISBN 1-58062-010-8
1. Adult child abuse victims—Psychology. 2. Boys—Abuse of—
Psychological aspects. 3. Psychologically abused men. 4. Adult child
abuse victims—United States—Psychology. I. Title.
HV6626.5.S68   1998
362.73'4'081—dc21   97-47497
                                              CIP

All of the cases and examples presented in this book are taken from actual patient material. In
each case the names, locations, and identifying details have been changed. In some examples
I created a composite of several patients' stories.

This publication is designed to provide accurate and authoritative information with regard to
the subject matter covered. It is sold with the understanding that the publisher is not engaged
in rendering legal, accounting, or other professional advice. If legal advice or other expert
assistance is required, the services of a competent professional person should be sought.
        — From a *Declaration of Principles* jointly adopted by a Committee of the
American Bar Association and a Committee of Publishers and Associations

Cover design by Mike Stromberg
Interior design by Richard Oriolo

This book is available at quantity discounts for bulk purchases.
For information, call 1-800-872-5627 (in Massachusetts 781-767-8100).

Visit our home page at http://www.adamsmedia.com

832240

Contents

8355.10

Acknowledgments

This book would have not been possible if not for the support and assistance of those around me.

First and foremost I would like to acknowledge my agent, Mary Yost, who saw this book from conception to delivery. Her patience, encouragement, and feedback has been a crucial factor in my developing confidence as a writer. I also want to thank her for directing me to my writing coach, Randy Greene, who helped me to develop my skills as a writer and access my own inner editor. Most importantly, I want to thank Roy Carlisle for his excellent editorial suggestions and Naomi Lucks for her excellent copyediting.

Most importantly, I would like to thank my editor at Adams Media Corporation, Pam Liflander, for her support and enthusiasm for this project.

I particularly want to thank my clients who read the manuscript prior to publication and gave me their valuable feedback. These men, as well as others whom I have met through my work, have helped me understand their wounds as well as my own and what was needed to bring about healing. You have opened your hearts to me and in doing so have inspired this book. Thank you.

Finally I would like to thank my partner in life, Mindy, whose unending love, support, patience, and acceptance has made it possible for me to heal my own wounds in a safe place—our marriage. She has been the source of valuable feedback and inspiration both during the good times and the painful moments. Mindy was there when I first thought of writing this book, and she has encouraged me all along the way. Thank you.

Foreword

The book you are about to read, *WOUNDED BOYS, HEROIC MEN*, will change your life forever if you or someone you care about has been abused.

It is impossible to turn on the television news or pick up a newspaper today without being faced with the consequences of uncontained violence. The toll of child abuse has a direct effect on the individuals involved and society as a whole. Less well perceived is the more indirect impact of abuse against children; the psychological pain and suffering that effects every aspect of the growing child's and adult's life, whether or not that person is aware of the connection.

Dr. Daniel Sonkin makes this connection for men who were wounded as boys. He helps men name their pain, explore their often buried abusive experiences, and then heal the wounds and change their lives so the tragedy of child abuse no longer controls them.

In my work with battered women and children, I am often asked why there are so many programs designed to help women heal from the abuse that victimizes them, while the men responsible are not provided with adequate treatment opportunities. Although there are many answers to that question, the most important response is that traditional psychotherapy has not been adequate to remediate the effects from abuse. Men must first understand that they have been emotionally wounded by the abuse they have witnessed or experienced. It took the integration of feminist therapy theory politically exploring the effects of men's misuse of power and abuse on women and the new theories on trauma which created a therapy exploring the effects of abuse on both men and women to uncover, understand, and assist in the healing from violence experienced by women. The same combination of theories, those advocating equality between men and women as well as those dealing with the special mental health effects of trauma, are needed to help wounded men heal.

When I first met Daniel Sonkin in the late 1970's, he like many of us, was searching for answers to the devastation of family violence. It took only a little encouragement for him to become one of the trail-blazers and foremost authorities in the treatment of abusive men. From this work, he recognized the impact of child abuse and its role in the perpetuation of various forms of abuse within our society. While abuse often does beget more abuse, and men who abuse women were often abused themselves as children, being damned to commit future violence is not the only legacy received by child abuse victims. Like other trauma victims, many men are doomed to repeat their own experiences, sometimes in reality and sometimes in dreams and night terrors. Others must block their feelings, through both chemical and psychological means, to protect themselves from the awful truths they fear to remember. The cost in destroyed human relationships, aborted careers, and lives not fully lived is a very high price indeed. But, the optimistic message in this book is that recovery of one's fullest potential is indeed possible.

Those of us in the woman's movement have been looking for the other side of the revolution to begin. We know that unless men reach their fullest potential through their own efforts, women will continue to have to take care of them if we want positive relationships with men. Unless men become proud of themselves and learn to trust women to care about them without taking over women's lives with power and control tactics, violence will continue to be a resource for some men to force women to meet their needs. If one man beats up just one woman or child, none of us will be safe. True equality between men and women is possible if both men and women learn to live together without anger, abuse, and violence. The message you will get from these pages will help you gain the skills needed to live together in harmony and peace.

Lenore E. A. Walker, Ed.D., ABPP
Diplomate in Clinical Psychology
Denver, Colorado
April, 1992
Author of: *The Battered Woman* and *Terrifying Love: Why Battered Women Kill and How Society Responds.*

Introduction: Child Abuse and You

For the past twenty-five years, researchers, clinicians, activists, and courageous survivors of abuse have helped to lift the shroud of secrecy covering the serious problems of physical, sexual, and psychological maltreatment of children. As a result of these efforts, the general public has also become more conscious of the prevalence as well as the destructiveness of child abuse. Self-help books, like the *Courage to Heal*, newspaper and magazine articles, and feature movies, such as *Shine,* are contributing to a new public awareness of child abuse and it's potentially devastating effects on child development. Television talk shows bring into our living rooms survivors and perpetrators of horrific abuse who psychologically bleed before our very eyes. Gruesome high-profile murders continually remind us of the sometimes lethal and desperate outcome of years of undetected abuse.

For most of these years that society has been confronting the problem of child abuse, the persons who have received the most focus are female victims of abuse. This is in part related to the fact that the majority of victims of sexual abuse are females. But statistics about physical and psychological abuse indicate more egalitarian trends. Today, more men are coming forward to talk about their experiences with physical, psychological, and sexual abuse.

As a society, we have become much more aware of this problem, yet we are still far from understanding the real meaning of being abused, its long-term effects, and effective solutions. This fact is most evident in the legal system where contradictions abound. For example, as a society, we deplore child abuse and will do anything to protect victims, yet, when prosecuting and punishing perpetrators, there is little understanding and consideration for these adults who were once themselves victims of abuse. There exists tremendous social pressure from communities for judges to dispense the most severe sentences possible for perpetrators of abuse without any consideration for the possibility for rehabilitation. On the other hand, it is not unusual for judges to also be pressured by father's rights activists and as a result ignore the potential for harm to the children and give alleged perpetrators of abuse full physical custody or unsupervised visitation during divorce proceedings.

This contradiction also exists with the death penalty. Most people sitting on death row were themselves the victims of the most severe forms of child abuse. Few, if any, had any chance of being protected by society and, therefore, grew up learning to do as their abusers did—hurt and exploit others. Few people have any understanding or compassion for these adult perpetrators. The solution, the death penalty, is revenge and once again the abused are powerless to change their fate. But who punishes *their* abusers?

In the past five years, there has been a tremendous upsurge of organizations formed to protect persons accused of child abuse, such as the False Memory Syndrome Foundation. These organizations have been in part a reaction to what seems to be a witch hunt for child abusers, but more specifically in reaction to some well-meaning (some people would question this characterization), but unskilled, therapists inappropriately convincing patients that they were abused as children when in fact the patients have no specific memories of abuse. When considering the power of persuasion, therapists are in a position wielding tremendous influence over their patients, who already are vulnerable because of their emotional problems. We go to counselors not only to find solutions to problems, but in many cases to understand the origin of those problems. In the song "Officer Krupke," *West Side Story*, the Jets sing about why they have problems with delinquency—family, social, psychological—we can now add to the list, a victim of child abuse. Unfortunately, human behavior can not be simply reduced to one experience or another. As I discuss in this book, you may have certain symptoms today that are similar to problems experienced by many survivors of abuse. However, your difficulties may be caused from your experiences of child abuse or may be a result of other experiences. Most importantly, I do not suggest that you assume you were abused as a child if you do not have any memories of such abuse. Although, there is research that indicates some abused persons may actually have forgotten or repressed the memory of the abuse, just having many of the symptoms described in the book, yet no recollection of abuse, doesn't mean memories have been repressed. However, even if you have memories of abuse, do not assume that your problems are a direct result of abuse. Personally, I do not think it is always important to figure out this distinction. What is most important is that if you are suffering today, you need to find a way of dealing with it. Because we can not change the past, it is best to focus much of our efforts on today and the future.

On a positive note, over the past seventeen years, self-help and professional resources have been developed so that mental health counselors have more effective and compassionate responses to both victims and perpetrators of abuse. This book includes many of those approaches.

What About You?

If you were physically, sexually, or psychologically abused as a boy, this book is for you. Use it as a guide in your attempt to overcome the negative long-term effects of your abusive experiences. It is also a guide to help your partner, friends, and family members better understand your struggles and ultimately support you in your healing journey. This book will not label you as defective, screwed up, or somehow less of a man. On the contrary, I believe that it takes a hero to admit to being hurt or having problems and to take the risk of asking for help and changing unhealthy patterns of behavior.

As you read about the pain and suffering associated with child abuse, please remember that redemption and healing are possible. If you have experienced abuse in any of its forms, you don't have to live with your secret any longer. You can talk about your experiences. You can get in touch with powerful feelings that you have carried on your shoulders for so many years. You can wake up each day feeling more in control of your life, less tense, more self-aware, and ultimately enjoy greater happiness and peace of mind.

My message is simple: Get help! Old patterns will resist change, therefore having a person or persons whom you trust can be of great assistance as you continue on your healing journey. Counseling can be a safe place where you can develop the strength to talk about your feelings and experiences with a person who understands your inner pain. Although your impulse will be to solve your problems on your own, *you can't do it alone*.

Fight that impulse to do it by yourself. This will only prolong the process and may in fact make it even more difficult. You are not the first person to take this journey. Benefit from the wisdom of others. The work that you do in your healing is of heroic proportions. It may be the greatest challenge you encounter in your life. It will frequently feel very difficult, and at times may seem impossible. With the help of others you will be better prepared to face your own demons.

Your payoff for entering the lion's den is many-sided: You will eventually feel a greater peace of mind with yourself. You will be better able to weather the problems that life deals you. You will have more energy for living. You will ultimately be happier. You will bring greater joy to the people around you. These will be the fruits of your labor. Good luck on your journey.

WOUNDED BOYS, HEROIC MEN

Chapter 1

WOUNDED MEN, WOUNDED BOYS

The first time Sam called my office to make an appointment his voice was soft but urgent. He said that he needed to see me immediately. He had a real problem: his wife had given him an ultimatum—"Either get into counseling or get a lawyer"—and then she had walked out. Two days later, when I opened the door to let him into the office, I was surprised to see a 250-pound man who looked like a guard for the San Francisco 49ers.

He seemed reluctant and angry as he entered my office, and I had the feeling he was not there by choice. I asked him to set on the sofa. He sat down, crossed his arms on his chest, and crossed his legs. His expression challenged me, as if saying, Okay. Do your thing, Doc.

Sam was probably feeling the same way I did during my first session in a therapist's office; I didn't know what to say or expect. So I made nothing of his defensive posture. Instead, I asked, "Have you ever been to a counselor before?"

"Just once with my wife, but not alone," he said. "In fact I've always figured that therapy was for people who were a little crazy. My wife was seeing a therapist because one of her friends was seeing one. That's probably how all the trouble started in the first place, and now I'm here."

"Many men who enter into therapy for the first time think the same thing," I responded, and tried to reassure him that I didn't think that he was crazy. "People seek a therapist's help for many reasons. Usually they're just looking for help with a personal problem from a person who can present them with a fresh point of view."

He breathed a sigh of relief, unfolded his arms, and uncrossed his legs. I asked, "What specifically brings you here today?"

"My wife left me this weekend. We've been fighting a lot lately and I think she's just had it with me and my temper."

I asked about his temper.

"I want to be left alone when I get angry," he responded, "so I go off by myself. My wife follows me and keeps pushing my buttons. She says, 'Talk to me. You never talk to me.' Then I get so mad I begin to talk to her. But it's more like yelling. I kind of rant and rave. After a while I just calm down."

I asked how his wife felt about his going off by himself.

"I don't know," he said. "Frustrated, I suppose. If she doesn't like it she should just leave me alone."

I asked a similar question about his yelling.

"I don't know. Maybe she gets pissed off," he said. "She says she gets scared."

Why, I asked, did he think she felt that way?

"I think her father used to beat her up pretty badly."

"And have you ever felt like hitting her?"

He said emphatically, "It's crossed my mind a couple of times."

Then I asked if he had ever done that.

"Well, once before," he said, cutting off his words.

"Can you talk about it?"

During what was a long pause, I noticed that Sam was quite uncomfortable talking about what happened. He probably had never told anyone about the violence. So I said, "I know talking about these problems can feel embarrassing. But maybe I can help you understand your situation from a different perspective so that you can approach your problems differently. Maybe you would feel better just to talk about it. That's what counseling is really all about. Tell me what happened."

"Well," he began, "about five years ago I was drinking heavily and we got into a big fight about her family's visiting. She's very close with them—always talking to them on the phone and going to visit." He paused, as if the memory were becoming clearer in his mind, then added, "I had just come home from work and had had a really bad day. Before she even asked me about my day she came right up to me and told me she had already invited them to come visit us for two weeks. I said okay, but inside I knew it wasn't. I just got real quiet. I guess you might say I started moping around the house." Suddenly his tone became almost confessional. "Then I was slamming doors, throwing things down. I wasn't very nice to her. I was in the bedroom watching the news and she came in to talk. She starting asking me how I was feeling. Once she started seeing this therapist, she was always asking me, 'How do you feel?' I don't know how the fuck I feel! So I just ignored her."

At this point Sam's eyes became intense, and his voice grew angry as he remembered. "Finally she was right up in my face telling me if I wasn't going to communicate with her that there was no point being together. The next thing I knew I was on top of her, screaming as loud as I could. I had my hands around her neck and I was choking her. I mean I wasn't really choking her, but I was holding her down." Then the confessional tone returned. "I know that there's no excuse for it, but it was a bad time for me at work and she got real angry at me, accusing me of not wanting her family to visit."

I asked him if there had been some truth to that statement.

"I guess so," he said. "I'm not very close to my own family and I felt a little jealous of her relationship with hers."

"What happened afterward?"

"We didn't talk all night and most of the next day. And then we just kind of forgot about it."

"We?"

"Well, I tried to."

I challenged him to think about whether or not she wanted to forget about the fight.

"Not from the sound of this letter she left me."

Sam's way of resolving the argument was by promising never to do it again. And although he never physically abused her again, he would frequently abuse her psychologically with threats and put-downs. They went to a counselor together. Sam talked about his alcoholic father, who also had a violent temper. The therapist recommended that Sam get into counseling as well. As far as Sam was concerned, his father was history. Like many men who were abused, he couldn't see how digging up the past would change the present. Sam was convinced that if Carol would just back off he wouldn't get so mad. He agreed to make a few calls to the therapists but always found reasons for not going, the best being money. After a while Carol just stopped nagging him about it. He came home last Friday after work and found this note:

Dear Sam,

I can't live with your anger anymore. I've been waiting three years for you to get help and you always have had an excuse not to go to therapy. I'm not exactly sure why you are so afraid to look at your childhood, but I guess that something happened that was very hurtful and frightening. I know that whatever happened then is still hurting you today. I have tried talking about it, I've tried ignoring it, I've tried being understanding and patient. Nothing seems to help. You are either cold, distant, and withdrawn, or you're exploding out of control. I can't get close to you. I am still scared that you will become violent with me again. I can't live with your pain and rage any longer. I can tell you are avoiding having contact with me. You're either at work, fixing something around the house, out with your friends, or drinking and watching television. Please get help before you hurt yourself or someone else. I want you to know that I am safe and will call in about a week, after I have had some time to sort things out for myself.

Love, Carol

I asked him what he thought she meant when she said "something happened that was very hurtful and frightening."

Sam lowered his head onto his hand and rested his elbow on the armrest of the couch. There was a long silence. His voiced quivered as he replied, "I don't know why this is important."

"It's only important if whatever happened yesterday still gets in the way of your life today."

"I don't know if that's true."

I asked him if he was willing to find out.

"Why is this so fucking important?" His tone of his voice noticeably changed to anger. "It's my marriage that's falling apart."

His face was turning red and he was pounding his fist on the armrest as he spoke. This calm man was beginning to transform before my eyes. No matter how important I thought it was that he face his demons, we weren't going to get anywhere unless he thought so as well. I wanted to help him get through these powerful emotions, so I asked him how he was feeling right now, hoping that he didn't think I was sounding like his wife.

"I'm fine."

"Then I'd like you to take a minute to check in with how your body is feeling. How do your arms and hands feel? How about your chest and stomach? What about your head and neck? What are your physical sensations?"

Sam quietly reflected on these questions. I could tell that he was focusing his attention to the various parts of his body. He looked up and said, "I'm kind of tense in my stomach and my shoulders."

"And as you were asking me, 'Why is this so fucking important?' what were you doing with your body? Was there a change in your tone of voice?" I hoped that helping him get in touch with the physical and behavioral signs of his emotions would make it easier for him to identify his anger.

"Yeah, I guess I was pounding my fist, and I raised my voice."

I asked what he was feeling at that moment.

"Maybe I was beginning to feel a little pissed off."

"About what?"

"Well, I guess I didn't like hearing that I needed to talk about my family stuff." He paused, then added with emphasis, "You're the third person to tell me that. I don't think it's that important. But I am about to lose my marriage, so I'm willing to do anything to stop that from happening."

Sam's story is typical of many men who were victims of childhood abuse. His life is troubled and he feels that it's beyond his control. He is not so much interested in seeking personal help for himself as he is trying to "fix" his marriage. He has a great deal of difficulty identifying and communicating his feelings. He doesn't see the importance of talking about his childhood experiences and how they may have been partly the cause of his problems today. Like many men, Sam is not clear about how therapy works and why it can be useful in solving problems. Like many wounded men, Sam has a pain inside that he tries not to think about or feel. But when someone starts to ask specific questions about what happened in his childhood, how he felt then and how he feels now, he begins to drop his guard and many of those old feelings rush in.

After several sessions Sam was finally able to acknowledge that he had been abused as a boy. His father beat him with a belt, a stick, or whatever was convenient, and Sam frequently had welts on his back, bottom, and legs. He refused to go swimming or wear shorts during the summer for fear that others would see his injuries. And his father's violence was not restricted to him. Sam frequently watched his father physically abuse his mother. The son could not recall a week passing without his father coming home drunk and getting into a fight with his mother. Typically his father slapped his mother and pushed her around. On several occasions Sam remembered his father choking his mother unconscious. Sam also recalled being so fearful of his father that he couldn't move. This is Sam's most vivid memory:

> One night I was watching TV after a tense dinner. We were all walking on eggshells trying not to get Dad upset. He used to get real angry if anyone would scrape their plate with their fork or knife. All I could think about was not making a single noise. I was so focused on my plate that I don't even remember anything anyone said. I learned how to shut the world out. Anyway, the inevitable happened. Someone said or did something wrong and he went crazy. He grabbed my mother by the hair and dragged her into the living room. He was beating the shit out of her. I was so terrified all I could do was keep looking at my plate so as to not make any noise. I glanced toward the living room briefly to see him choking her. Her entire face was blue. I couldn't move. I was terrified. What would he do to me if I tried to stop him? I looked back at my plate and just keep eating.

As a result of these and other experiences Sam felt a great deal of anger, rage, and hurt. But he never expressed those feelings because it was neither safe nor encouraged. Therefore he never learned how to deal with these or other intense emotions in an appropriate way. Instead he would stuff them deep inside, hoping they would never show their ugly heads. Because he had no healthy way to ventilate these strong emotions he would resort to the violence that he learned as a boy helped when feeling intense anger, hurt, or fear. Whenever conflict would arise in his marriage, a flood of strong emotions would immediately surface. One time his anger led to physical violence, but more often he would become verbally abusive and intimidating.

Sam also told me that there were times when he felt as if he was "being possessed" by his feelings: "When we first started talking about the abuse, I would leave your office with this sick feeling in the bottom of my stomach. It was twisting, wrenching. It was as if I was a wet towel being wrung. Sometimes I would be sitting quietly or at my work and I would begin to think about what happened. Then I'd panic. I felt possessed by these intense feelings. All I could do to stop myself from screaming was to distract myself. Five o'clock never came soon enough." This is a common reaction early in the healing process. As old memories begin to surface you are also likely to feel the old emotions associated with the abuse.

These intense feelings were present even when Sam was mad. His wife, Carol, felt his anger just by living under the same roof with him. His friends, coworkers, and other family members also sensed anger within him. In order for Sam to heal from the abuse he needed to acknowledge the presence of these powerful feelings within himself. Sam needed to admit that he was a wounded man.

Sam's therapy led him to realize the effects the old abuse had on today's feelings, attitudes, and behaviors. The initial work of uncovering the memories was very difficult, but over time the intensity of the feelings lessened. Soon he was not only able to talk openly about the abuse but he became better able to recognize when those feelings and attitudes of yesterday were affecting his feelings and attitudes toward his partner today. After six months' separation he and his wife entered couples counseling and three months later began to live with each other again.

The Wounded Man

If you were physically beaten, sexually abused, or psychologically maltreated as a boy, it is important for you to realize that you are not alone. There are hundreds of thousands of others like you. Many of these men have already successfully healed their inner

Childhood abuse and destructive behaviors are not strictly male problems. Research in the area of child sexual abuse indicates that the majority of victims are female. The reason for this trend is that females have historically been devalued in our society, and as a result have been exploited sexually by men. On the other hand, male children seem to be more often victims of physical abuse. One theory to explain this has to do with the belief that male children can take greater physical punishment than females. Also, some fathers believe that beating their son will make him more of a man when he grows up. As a result of these experiences boy and girls become wounded in many similar ways. But because of differences in the way men and women are raised, their anger and low self-esteem may manifest themselves in distinctly different behaviors. Girls are taught to take responsibility for the success or failure of relationships. Therefore, many women turn their anger inward, which results in depression. Men are encouraged to solve problems by manipulating the environment and therefore tend to turn their anger outward, which may result in controling and abusing others. In either case, the wounds that were caused by childhood abuse need to be brought out into the open and healed so that these negative patterns are replaced by healthier ways of coping with difficult emotions that we all feel at times.

wounds. These wounds cannot be detected with X rays or blood tests; they are wounds of the soul, the spirit—the psyche.

If you have a great deal of inner hurt and rage stemming from childhood abuse, you are a wounded man. Ironically, as a wounded man, you may not know that you are feeling these emotions because you did not learn how to identify and communicate your feelings in a positive, productive way. Or you may have even learned to split off from your feelings altogether, as a way of coping with these strong emotions. But these powerful feelings don't go away by themselves. They need an outlet. You're like a pressure cooker: If you don't let the steam out, you'll explode.

Explosions of intense emotion are common for wounded men who haven't learned how to express their feelings in constructive ways. Unless you deal with the pressure directly, destructive behaviors are inevitable. These behaviors are destructive because they will continue to cause more problems in your life. Such problems include depression, violence, and alcoholism or drug addiction. In order to change these unhealthy behavior patterns you must directly address the wound itself.

Wounded men are hurt, injured, and confused inside. If a broken finger isn't properly set by a doctor, the bone will set itself improperly. It may just look bent and be a reminder about the time you broke your finger; or you may realize that something is wrong with the way that finger feels and works. And even though the injury may not stop you from appearing "perfectly normal" to most people, you may develop an unusual way of using your hand to compensate. You have learned to adjust to your injury. But what happens when that finger is stressed? It may feel unusually painful or it may become even more vulnerable to breaking again. You may have learned to adjust to your emotional injuries in the same way. Unlike physical injuries, however, psychological injuries are much easier to hide. Yet psychological wounds linger in the back of your mind and remain dormant until you are confronted with a stressful situation that reactivates them.

The Wounding of Male Children

This year over 1.5 million children will experience some form of emotion, sexual, or physical abuse, and at least half of these will be boys. But no matter what type of abuse a boy experiences, the physical and psychological pain that it causes may result in many different types of problems throughout his life. Most commonly, the grown man continues to abuse himself and those closest to him.

Many adults say, "Boys are flexible. They can handle it." Or "Kids forget about it when they grow up." My interviews with hundreds of men abused as children, however, have not shown these statements to be true. In fact, the majority of these child victims of abuse have suffered for years. Many have numerous physical ailments, frequent nightmares, troubled interpersonal relationships, and serious behavior problems. Though many men try to forget their childhood experiences, the memories and their associated feelings still affect their lives.

Only in the last few years have counselors begun to understand male victims of child abuse. Men are now beginning to overcome social pressure that demands they be mentally and emotionally strong and seem unaffected by their pain. Women are helping men overcome these social pressures by encouraging them to express their weaknesses and vulnerabilities. Fifty years ago it was considered unmanly to cry. Today men are hearing from women and other men that it is okay to show their feelings. Many women now view it as a sign of strength when a man shows his emotions.

Abuse may carry a particularly high price for men. Males perpetrate the majority of abuses, and males perpetuate the generational cycle of violence. In order to stop the cycle of violence, you need to heal yourself. In doing so you not only help yourself but you contribute to a much-needed change in society. Today millions of adult male victims of child abuse suffer within themselves, and many cause suffering in others. By bringing an end to your own pain, you are more likely to do the same for others—whether it's your child, your spouse, a sibling, a friend, a parent, or someone you touch professionally. Healing is contagious. When one person does it, it inspires others to do the same.

Am I a Wounded Man?

How do you know if you are a wounded man? Start with the obvious—your *behaviors*. Do you have an explosive temper at home or at work? Do you have a difficult time making a commitment in an intimate relationship? Is there a lot of conflict in your marriage? Are you addicted to sex? Do you have an extreme fear of homosexuality or do you question your own sexual orientation? Do you frequent prostitutes? Do you have a drinking or a drug problem? Do you have trouble remaining sexually faithful in your relationship? Have you been violent with your spouse, partner, or children? Do you have other addictive patterns in your life?

Another way to determine if these invisible wounds exist inside yourself is to look at your *attitudes* toward yourself and others. What do you think of yourself as a man? What do you like and dislike about yourself? Most people don't consciously take the time to examine their strengths and shortcomings. Wounded men often have a poor self-image or low self-esteem. They are often critical of themselves and others. A good clue to how you feel about yourself is to think about how you treat others, especially those with whom you are intimate or emotionally close. For example, if you verbally insult your partner, you probably grew up with a critical parent. I wouldn't be surprised to find that you are also very critical with yourself. Another attitude to examine is trust. Do you trust others? Do you think that people close to you would hurt you if they knew how you thought or felt? Betrayal or trust is one of the outcomes of childhood abuse. A trusted adult uses his or her greater strength and power to take advantage of the child. As a result of this betrayal the young child grows up distrusting others, especially those close to him. How would you rate your self-esteem? What are your attitudes about trust?

A third area to look at is *feelings*. Do you know how you feel most of the time? Many wounded men lack awareness of their feelings. As a result they are unable to communicate with others. On the other hand, you may be very aware of your feelings. In fact, you may be overwhelmed by their intensity and confused because so many different types of feelings surface at one time. Men who experience these intense emotions usually find ways to anesthetize themselves. You may use alcohol and drugs to avoid feelings, but any compulsive behavior—whether it's work, sex, eating, or withdrawal into a private world—can serve the same purpose. It helps you run away from your personal problems. How well do you deal with your feelings? How do you avoid your feelings?

Problems in any one of these areas may mean that the abuse you experienced as a child is still effecting you today. Being abused as a boy, however, may not be the only reason for these difficulties in your life. The problems may be compounded by the fact that the way boys are brought up in our society actually predisposes them to any one or a number of the issues described above.

Our experience as men is uniquely different from women's in two very important ways: an emphasis on thinking rather than feeling, and praise for using aggression and violence. Abused or not, the way most boys are raised in this society can predispose us to serious problems as adults, especially in relationships.

First, from birth on, men are taught to use the "thinking mode" far more than the "feeling mode," to be "rational" rather than "irrational": to be emotional is to act like a girl or a sissy. Men also learn that reason and logic are the best skills for success.

Rob, a forty-year-old lawyer, recently came to me because of his problem with alcoholism. He was raised by his alcoholic grandparents because his mother and his father abandoned him at an early age. Rob's wife had just left him, and I ask how he felt about it.

He looked at me with a blank stare and replied, "How do I feel? I think she should come back to me!" This man responded by using his thinking mode. He "thought" that she should come back to him. In order to help him get in touch with his feelings I asked a series of questions. The first was, "When you 'think' about her leaving you, what changes do you notice in your body?"

After several minutes of concentration, he replied, "I get tense in my stomach."

I then asked, "If that tension in your stomach had a voice, what would it say?"

"Come back, I miss you, I need you."

Next I asked him to say, "I'm scared, I am hurting."

He repeated "I'm scared and I am hurting" several times, then he turned to me and said, "Yes, that's it, that's right." At that point Rob was beginning to learn the language of feelings.

Because men are often uncomfortable with their feelings, they have great difficulty solving interpersonal problems constructively. When emotional difficulties arise they struggle—often unsuccessfully—to find a solution by using only logic. Men sometimes lack the flexibility to resolve their deepest feelings through introspection

The Wounds in All Men

"Thinking" versus "Feeling"

and communication. The result is that men frequently try to think their feelings away, try to find the logic in their emotions, or, most commonly, try to find an external cause for the problem.

Think about a time when your partner was trying to tell you her feelings. What was your response? Your first instinct was probably to try to understand *why* she was feeling that way or *how* you could make her feel better. If you didn't see the logic in her feelings you probably got frustrated. She may then have accused you of "not understanding." You may have tried even harder to talk her out of her feelings. And then an argument may be exploded, seemingly out of nowhere. This all happens because we feel uncomfortable with feelings. When we "think" that we have found the cause for our discomfort, namely another person, than we often attempt to get that person to change, or stop doing whatever we think it is that makes us feel uncomfortable. The problem with this strategy is that it never addresses the real problem of our discomfort with feelings. To compound the problem the other person experiences our response as controlling, not listening, and unsupportive.

When we use the thinking mode exclusively, rather than in combination with the feeling mode, we tend to devalue other people's feelings. This is why men have trouble communicating with women. It is as if we speak different languages. Women typically want to discuss their feelings, while men don't understand what the problem is. Men want to give advice. But women get angry because they don't want advice; they just want their feelings to be heard and accepted.

For centuries society has not given approval for men to experience and express their feelings, nurturing, relationship-oriented sides. Although men and women have the capacity to act in both traditionally masculine and feminine ways, boys and girls are saddled with sex-role expectations from birth. And such expectations limit their abilities to experience the full range of human potential.

Thus an important part of our healing process is to accept the various aspects of our inner selves, both masculine and feminine. When we achieve inner balance we are able to respond in a flexible way to situations outside ourselves. If a situation calls for a feeling response, then we are free to respond in that way. If it needs a thinking response, then we can think.

Tom, a thirty-eight-year-old, self-employed contractor, came to counseling in the midst of his divorce. This tall, thin, well-dressed man came into counseling on the advice of a friend. He was continually anxious and unable to sleep, relax, or concentrate on work. He had been severely psychologically abused by his father, who never showed him any physical affection. As far back as Tom could remember his father told him that to cry or show any emotion was being a sissy. Tom grew up the epitome of the thinking man. Feelings were simply not a part of his repertoire.

This wasn't too much of a problem until he married a very emotional woman. The more emotional she got, the more analytical he became. He felt intimidated by her feelings and responded by becoming even more analytical and emotionally distant. Over time he became estranged from his wife and found himself out of love with her. Eventually his wife left him. Now, for the first time in his life, Tom began to feel something. But these feelings were so intense that he didn't know how to verbalize them. I told Tom that this was an opportunity for him to get in touch with his feelings, to learn how to deal with a part of himself that his father had never allowed him to experience.

It took a major crisis for Tom to let himself feel strong emotions. Over time he became more and more comfortable using his feeling mode when the situation called for such a response. Such a crisis is often the factor that propels men into facing their emotions. If you are in a similar state you can learn how to make use of your feeling mode in all areas of your life. Uncomfortable situations arise in our lives to teach us lessons. And until we learn the task at hand they will keep coming up over and over again. When a wounded man refuses to face this challenge the crisis can become very frightening.

Men and Aggression   A second difference between men and women is that, from an early age, males are taught to use aggression and violence.

As infants boys are handled more roughly than girls. Boys are encouraged to participate in "rough-and-tumble" play. As we get older and are able to utilize our "thinking mode," we are encouraged to solve problems using logic and common sense. However, if that approach doesn't work, most males don't automatically switch to the feeling mode; instead, they usually resort to force.

Fighting is a "skill" every boy either develops or at least confronts while growing up. We have to prove manhood by demonstrating our physical strength. Fighting becomes a rite of passage. If we don't go out there and pick a fight, one will eventually come our way. Fighting also has rules. The first rule is: You should never walk away from a fight. If you do walk away, you are a coward, a sissy, or what is worse, according to the rules, acting like a girl. The second rule is: If you fight and get hurt, you shouldn't cry, because only girls cry. Showing hurt is not a boy's alternative; there is no alternative but to tough it out. And this rule is enforced by male role models from TV, movies, sports, and music, who give boys the same message: Be tough, be aggressive, and show strength.

How does this emphasis on aggression manifest if you experienced abuse as a child? As you begin to look inward you discover a great deal of hurt and anger. But society hasn't given you a vehicle to express your inner feelings, so you try to think them away or just to ignore them, or, worse, turn the situation around to match violence with violence. Social conditioning makes men prone to act out their feelings rather than communicate them, so you may be more likely to act on your aggressive impulses. Why? Because that's what you learned as a child.

The potential for aggressive responses to stressful situations is great for the wounded man. To say to yourself, "I'll never be like him [or her]" or, if you have already been abusive toward others, to tell yourself, "I'll never do it again" is not enough to bring about a change in your life. You need to go beyond words and face your inner feelings, develop new attitudes toward yourself and others, and learn new skills in dealing with personal problems. It is imperative that you actively begin to heal yourself. The healing process described in the book will help you bring about these changes.

Is Healing Possible?

Healing is possible. It will take some time and work. Many men and women in the helping professions have found methods that have been effective in helping men overcome the devastating effects of childhood abuse. I have personally watched hundreds of men rise above their wounds and find peace of mind. I like to think of these individuals are heroes because it takes a great deal of courage to go to battle with our inner demons.

It is very important for you to know that changing your patterns of behavior today does not totally depend on first healing all your childhood wounds. You can develop specific skills along the way to help you stop violence and substance abuse and resolve marital difficulties. But, in the long run, only by healing your inner wounds will you become able to prevent such serious behavior problems from reoccurring.

The Phases of the Healing Process

The process of healing your wounds from childhood abuse will, in many ways, be unique to your particular situation. However, four phases of healing are common to all men embarking on this journey. Healing is not a linear process, so you may not experience each phase in the order given below. But throughout your healing you will experience one or more of these phases individually or simultaneously.

1. *Awareness and disclosure* of being a wounded man and unlocking the thoughts and feelings that go along with those wounds.
2. *Understanding* how and why the abuse occurred and ultimately how it affects you today.

3. *Learning new skills,* attitudes, and ways of relating to others.
4. *Transformation,* the process that allows the development of different aspects of yourself.

Each of these phases has qualities that are particularly important for you.

Phase One: Awareness and Disclosure

Awareness and disclosure mean acknowledging that you were abused as a child and accepting all the thoughts and feelings that go along with that fact.

We have many secrets that we keep from others. Some secrets are meant to be kept to ourselves. But the most damaging secrets are the ones that we fail to acknowledge, even to ourselves. This may be the case for you. The thought of facing the abuse is so uncomfortable that you may want to take the memories (and all the thoughts and feelings that accompany such memories) and lock them up in a trunk in a basement. You may do this consciously, or you may have done it so long ago that you have forgotten all about it. In either case, even though the trunk is locked, the secret will unconsciously control your thoughts, feelings, and behaviors. Once you acknowledge the abuse you will begin to take control. You will no longer be a victim of the secret.

Once you have acknowledged the abuse and the emotions to yourself, the next step is disclosure—telling someone else. One result of hiding the secret is that you may feel a certain amount of alienation. Wounded men often feel misunderstood, detached, or estranged from others. Saying "I was sexually abused" or "I feel angry at my father for physically abusing me" will have a cathartic effect for you. You are likely to feel an immediate release of inner pressure, as if a load has been removed from your chest. The disclosure process may involve telling friends or other family members of the abuse, although this does not mean you should blurt out your secret to everyone you meet. Telling your secret to a supportive person will help you feel less alone in the world.

Disclosure is not very different from the idea of confession; it is a cleansing process that helps you feel a sense of relief.

Eventually you may want to confront your abuser. But this should not happen until you have become quite comfortable with your own healing process.

Understanding goes beyond recognizing the long-term effects of the abuse. Answering the questions Why did the abuser act in that way? and What other problems were occurring for the person at the time? may be a part of this stage of your healing process. Most important, this stage involves the realization that *you were not to blame for the abuse.* You did not cause the abuse or allow it to happen in any way. It is up to adults to protect children; it is not the child's role to protect himself from adults. Developing a general understanding of why people abuse others—children in particular—can help you step back from your experience and view it from a different perspective.

Phase Two: Understanding

For example, after many sessions of anger and tears, Mark, a well-dressed fifty-two-year-old businessman who lived a fast-track life-style, was able to step back from his experience and understand why his father physically abused him:

> It was very difficult for me to get beyond my anger toward my father for beating me all during my childhood. When I would think of him I'd only feel anger. As I began to look at his life and the problems he had, I began to realize, first, it wasn't my fault and second, he abused everyone he came in contact with. He grew up with a violent, alcoholic father and he just never dealt with his own pain. During the year in therapy that I began to deal with this part of my life, I actually began to develop some compassion for him. He was a sick guy. As I did I felt less angry and really began to feel in my heart that it wasn't my fault. Then I knew that I was beginning to heal.

Phase Three: Learning New Skills

The learning process is based on the assumption that everyone, both men and women, wounded or not, can stand to pick up new skills, attitudes, and ways of relating to others. You may have been feeling very angry all your life about the abuse. You are now experiencing dysfunctional patterns in your own relationships but are doing nothing to change the present. You may have analyzed your past so completely that only an intellectual understanding of your childhood abuse and as a result you now use it as an excuse or justification for your current problems. For example, when confronted about his abusive behavior toward his child, one man stated, "Oh, I do that because my parents treated me in the same way." The childhood abuse becomes an excuse for current behavior rather than a reason to change. So you first need to learn that *change is possible*. No matter how long you have had a particular way of acting or thinking, with persistence and practice you can learn new skills and attitudes.

Phase Four: Transformation

The transformation process occurs as you work through the other stages of the healing process. Awareness, disclosure, understanding, and learning help to change your attitudes, emotional disposition, and behaviors. You may begin to notice these changes in yourself; more frequently, however, such changes are noticed first by others. You will hear friends make statements such as: "You have changed in the last year" or "You are less tense, less on edge lately" or "You have been expressing your feelings a lot more lately" or "You seem more self-confident than you did several years ago."

The transformation process also involves using the experience to cultivate other sides of yourself. For example, if you have a tendency to think and analyze your feelings away, then you may want to learn how to feel more comfortable with experiencing and communicating your emotions. Or, if you haven't learned to step back, deliberate, and understand your emotions, then you may need to develop your thinking skills. Men who find it easier to experience their anger may need to express their sadness more often. Extroverts who need constant attention from others may want to nurture their quiet side, becoming more comfortable with themselves.

Transformation occurs when you use the abusive experience as a springboard to enhance sides of your personality that may have been blocked. Sometimes this happens consciously, such as when the extrovert says to himself, "I am going to spend some time alone today," or when the thinking type asks himself, "How do I feel about this situation?" At other times transformation occurs unconsciously over time through the process of healing.

You may have transformed your experience in more obvious ways, such as getting involved with programs that help victims or offenders of violence. Maybe you have been attracted to a profession that encourages healing, such as psychology, religious studies, medicine, or other people-helping fields. You can help others with their pain if you are willing to work on yourself as well. If this is the case for you, it is important that you attend to your own wounds so they won't get in the way of your helping others.

As you are transformed you will find that you are less effected by the past and feel better about yourself and how you respond to others. It doesn't mean that you will never feel the pain again or that you won't encounter problems in your relationships. But it does mean that you will not let your childhood experiences determine your response to those problems. You will have more choices, fewer knee-jerk reactions. Therefore you will have greater control over yourself. Mark was physically abused by his mother. As a result he would become very defensive whenever a woman would criticize him. Now he can catch himself when this reaction occurs. He can say to himself, "She is not my mother and I am not a child. Is she saying something valid or do I need to assert myself?"

Ultimately your process of healing will be unique within this framework. Therefore your timing will be determined by your own inner readiness for any particular stage. That inner clock needs to be respected by counselors and family members as well as yourself. The choice to heal rests with you, and only you can decide when and how that will occur.

Three years ago, during the week of Father's Day, I asked each man in my wounded men's group to imagine that his father was there in the group. Each group member was to tell his father something he had never told him before. I placed an empty chair in the center of the circle: "There he is, your father. What do you want to say to him?"

The tension in the room increased tenfold. Each person began to express his thoughts and feelings. Barry, forty-five and unemployed, who had been referred to the group for physically abusing his daughter and wife, was unable to do the exercise. He said that he was afraid. When I asked him what he was afraid of, he stated, "If I got in touch with how I feel about this guy I might get violent." He wasn't ready for this exercise. He had only been dealing with these intense feelings for a few months. I told him it was okay for him to just watch and listen to the others. A year later I repeated the exercise. This time Barry was able to participate. He was ready to open up to his feelings.

For two more years Barry struggled to heal his wounds from childhood abuse. He had witnessed years of violence between his mother and father. His father physically abused him and sexually abused his younger sister. When he was ten years old his mother killed his father with a knife. She was found guilty of murder and was sent to jail, and he lived in one foster home after another until he was eighteen. He developed a serious drug problem as an adult, which let to three marriages and three divorces. In each marriage he was physically abusive. He came into counseling after attempting suicide when his third wife left him for another man. He saw no hope for his future.

At his first session he disclosed his mother's murder of his father. It was the first time in thirty-five years that he had talked about what happened. His rage toward his parents came up in every session. The hurt, fear, and pain were not far behind. The feelings seemed endless. Over time, however, they became less intense, less present and overbearing. Through his therapy he came to better understand his parents. He realized that he wasn't the cause of their problems. He wasn't to blame for the violence. Barry learned how the violence effected his own sense of self-esteem, and how he carried his rage into each of his marriages. He saw how he was blaming his wife for his pain, just as he was blaming himself for his parents' problems. Through his participation in the group Barry learned how to talk out his feelings and problems rather than act them out.

Over a period of three years Barry was transformed. To this day he still has anger and sadness about what happened in his family. But he's better able to recognize when those old feelings are getting in his way of seeing what is going on at the moment. He occasionally falls into old patterns, but he's able to catch himself before they get out of hand. He says, "The memories are a reminder that I need to be careful. I don't want to forget them altogether. Otherwise I may repeat the same mistakes. I've had enough abuse in my life."

Chapter 2

PREPARATION FOR YOUR JOURNEY

You must begin your healing journey with the right attitude. The healing process is very difficult, a challenge of heroic proportions. In order to make your own particular journey less traumatic I encourage you to make a conscious decision to approach the process with a healthy attitude.

The Right Attitude

How do you find the right attitude? The answer lies within letters of the word *HOW*: honesty, openmindedness, and willingness. These qualities are the key to healing your childhood abuse.*

*The concept of HOW (honesty, openmindedness and willingness) comes from Alcoholics Anonymous. AA uses many such slogans that help keep the process of understanding and working the Twelve Steps simple.

The first step in addressing any problem, whether it's healing from childhood abuse, stopping abusive behavior, or controlling addictions, is to be honest with yourself and eventually with others.

Honesty

Being honest begins with acknowledging the abuse and taking stock of how it affected you then and how it affects you today. It may be difficult for you to be honest in facing your vulnerabilities, weaknesses, and shortcomings or even to acknowledge that you have a problem. However, without honesty, the healing process is not possible.

Another aspect of honesty is to acknowledge your feelings, fantasies, and thoughts. You may have feelings of anger, hurt, and fear that may be difficult for you to recognize and communicate. You may have negative thoughts or fantasies, such as images of abusing others or yourself, that are painful or embarrassing to talk about. Through honesty the wound is exposed and healing begins. Talking out your feelings, thoughts, fantasies, and memories will also help remove your tendency to act them out in unhealthy or destructive ways.

Along the healing journey you will encounter new ideas, concepts, and suggestions that may seem foreign, illogical, or even absurd. There will be certain mental exercises to perform, which experience has shown me are helpful to men healing from childhood abuse. It is crucial to the healing process that you stay open and impartial and give equal weight to these new ideas even if you don't understand the point. In order for you to change you need to be open to new ways of being and break through rigid, dysfunctional ways of viewing yourself and others.

Openmindedness

First and foremost you need to be open to the idea that healing is possible for you. Second, and equally important, you must be open to the idea that your experience has not only caused you grief but presents you with an opportunity to learn to develop new aspects of yourself as well as new skills. Above all you need to be open to the notion that you are a hero. Breaking through old patterns of behavior takes persistence, strength, and the belief that the rewards are worth the effort. Don't forget, you have survived so far and can move on from survival to success. It is also necessary for you to be open to the fact that you are fundamentally a good person, no matter what type of problems you now experience. Through healing your problems will decrease, and the way you go about solving them will be more productive than in the past.

Willingness Initially you may feel that you are being forced to address this problem because of a failing marriage, alcoholism, or an arrest. You may begin to feel resentful that someone else is making you look at yourself in a way that brings up a great deal of pain, discomfort, or embarrassment. You will want to resist looking at this stuff; every man does at one point. It is important that you stay willing to stick with your journey even when the going gets rough. Because of your circumstances, willingness may begin as resignation; but over time you will become more inclined to want to change for you, not just for others.

Undoubtedly there will be times along your journey when you will want to give up and go back to old patterns. This is where your willingness will be most challenged. In Alcoholics Anonymous they talk about willingness to go to any lengths to become sober. This means voluntarily doing whatever it takes to solve your problem. The hero who embarks on the healing journey is challenged in a similar way. No matter how difficult the challenge, it is important for you to meet it squarely and move forward as much as possible.

The Rough Spots As you begin the healing process you are likely to encounter some difficult periods that may slow you down, stop you altogether, or create a backslide. You may begin to feel overwhelmed by your emotions, confusion and shock, guilt and shame, depression, agitation and anxiety, flashbacks and dreams, and the urge to slip back into denial. Expecting these junctures and preparing ahead of time can help you lessen their impact.

During your healing process you are likely to become acutely aware of the reservoir of emotions that lies silently—and sometimes not so silently—within you. As you begin to recognize your anger, sadness, hurt, and fear you may initially feel overwhelmed by emotions that have lain dormant for years. You may even fear that you will lose control, go crazy, or never feel good again once you begin to heal your wounds. Becoming aware of these intense feelings is an important part of healing. It will take you some time to get comfortable with them, but as you do, you will learn that they gradually decrease in intensity with time.

Emotions

You may experience confusion and shock when you first acknowledge that you were abused as a child. You may ask yourself, What do I do with this information? After such a disclosure it will take time for the dust to settle and for the direction of travel to become clearer. It is important to develop patience. Healing does not occur overnight.

Confusion and Shock

After you acknowledge or disclose your abuse you may experience guilt and shame. This is a common response.

Guilt and Shame

You may be feeling protective of your abuser, thinking, I don't want others to dislike him or him to feel uncomfortable. Or you may be worrying about the turmoil it may cause in the family: I don't want to cause problems with everyone. You may believe that somehow you brought this on yourself and may be feeling ashamed of yourself. These feelings are ways that you continue to blame yourself for the abuse. Guilt and shame will only prevent you from doing the work you need to do in order to heal. It is probable that others may get upset if they knew about what happened. Maybe they should.

Yes, your abuser may feel uncomfortable. But what about *your* feelings?

The bottom line is that *you are not to blame for the abuse*. And although talking about it may cause others to feel uncomfortable, you need to take care of yourself. You don't have control over other people's feelings and reactions. It may feel very painful for you and for them should you choose to disclose the abuse to family members. But you don't have to make that decision at this moment. Your protection of others is noble, but it may be at your own expense.

Depression Depression is another common response to acknowledging childhood victimization. You may have been already experiencing low-level depression before you began your healing process, but it may be exacerbated once the abuse is disclosed. The depression is often a result of anger that you long ago repressed or turned inward. The depression may also be a result of feeling helpless and powerless over uncomfortable feelings or situations. Like many men you probably like to feel in charge of your life, strong and in control. You may already be experiencing feelings of powerlessness and helplessness in your relationships and at work, stemming from the abuse. These feelings, along with the anger, sadness, and hurt, may be overwhelming and could cause depression.

Agitation and Anxiety Agitation and anxiety in the form of feeling nervous and being unable to sleep or concentrate on work may also occur in the early stages of healing. You may feel constantly on the edge of getting angry, irritable, or easily upset. Some wounded men find themselves obsessing about the abuse or other problems to the point that they can't get their work accomplished. Later in this book I will give specific suggestions on how to deal with anger constructively so that irritations and anxiety do not lead to abusive behavior.

Flashbacks and Dreams Flashbacks are intrusive memories about the abuse that may occur at any time. They may be very frightening and upsetting, but don't panic if you experience them. They are a normal part of the healing process, and it's even a good sign that these memories are beginning to surface. It shows that you're becoming more open to dealing with the abuse and, most important, you are more ready psychologically to move along in the healing process.

Most men are frustrated with their flashbacks because of their uncontrollability. That is, you can't control when, where, or if they are going to happen, although you can control what you do with them. One of my clients compared his dreams and flashbacks to the weather. We really can't control what the weather is going to be like today. All we can do is be prepared by listening to the forecast and having the right items in our possession (an umbrella for rain, a short-sleeved shirt for sun). If you have the right clothes and gear you will minimize your inconvenience and discomfort. In the same way, if you have the skills necessary to cope with feelings, dreams, and flashbacks, then the pain and anguish that accompany these experiences will be somewhat diminished. Inappropriate responses to these experiences can be as self-destructive as going out in the snow without shoes.

Dreams, like flashbacks, can also help or hinder the healing process depending on how you relate to them. Dreams can give you valuable information about your feelings, thoughts, and attitudes that can ultimately help you grow and learn more about yourself. If you consider yourself weak and crazy for having dreams, then you are not going to be open to using them to heal. On the other hand, if you are receptive and even welcome them, you will find them a valuable tool.

Denial

Slipping back into denial is a common tendency for most men in the process of healing. You'll most likely feel that talking about the abuse once or twice will be enough for you. And, in fact, it may be—but just for the moment. The desire to protect others may lead you to minimize the abuse or change your mind altogether, saying, "It really wasn't abuse."

Most men are task-oriented, and they like to know when the job is done. Unfortunately, the milestones of healing are not always easy to distinguish. If you want immediate results you are likely to convince yourself that you are now okay, or you may just give up the journey out of frustration. Faith in yourself is the strongest medicine you have for fighting these tendencies. You have to believe in your ability to heal and become the type of person you want to be.

As a child you probably felt on some level that the abuse was wrong. This voice was your inner wise old man trying to tell you that your perceptions were correct. It *was* abuse. Listening to that voice today will help you through the times when minimization and denial are strongest. The inner voice is what has gotten you this far in your healing journey.

Masculinity as a Help and as a Hindrance

"Masculinity" refers to certain qualities or characteristics our society expects of men that are, for the most part, not genetically predetermined but learned behaviors. These characteristics include being strong, aggressive, rough-natured, rational, brave, and independent. "Femininity" refers to qualities our society expects of women, such as being emotional, passive, empathic toward others, gentle, home-loving, relationship-oriented, and dependent. Because these qualities are learned, we all have a certain amount of both sex-type qualities within our personalities. In fact, more men and women today are changing these social prescriptions of expected behavior. Many women are aggressive, strong, rational, and independent; and increasing numbers of men express their gentle side and their emotions and are more home-loving and relationship-oriented. More and more people are struggling to reach a balance in their masculine and feminine qualities.

Masculinity and femininity are not inherently good or bad. Each has its place, depending on the situation. In fact, each consists of qualities that can help you in your healing process. For example, it takes a great deal of inner strength and discipline to embark on a healing journey, and when you are experiencing powerful emotions your rational function can serve you well. However, those masculine qualities alone will not be enough to heal your inner wounds. If you tend to lean too much toward the stereotypic masculine, you may be lacking in certain qualities that may help you in healing.

There are many feminine qualities that will help you through your healing journey. Allowing yourself to experience your emotional side will help you get through painful moments. When you let yourself be passive and sit quietly you can learn a lot about yourself. Listen to your inner thoughts, allow your feelings to surface, and pay attention to your dreams and fantasies. Empathy and compassion for yourself as well as others will help you to raise your self-esteem. When you permit yourself to depend on the help of others you will find healing progresses more rapidly than if you weather the pain all alone.

Striking a balance between masculinity and femininity can be one outcome of your healing journey. Throughout life we encounter situations that call for a particular response. Some situations require a more aggressive and rational reaction; others call for emotionality or reflection. Flexibility is the key to productive problem solving, and this is especially true for your healing journey.

Getting over the Rough Spots

There are a number of practical techniques for dealing with the rough spots and facilitating the healing process in general. You may want to try any one or a number of the following suggestions as you move along your journey. I have found professionally that a combination of recommendations works best. Some of these recommendations involve only yourself, some involve other people.

When You Feel Overwhelmed: Use the Feelings Log

The feelings log is simply a notepad in which you record your feelings. You may use a pocket size or standard-size pad, whichever is more convenient. Carry it with you every day and use it to write down incidents that stir up feelings and what those feelings are. It may be something someone said to you or something that they did. Feelings may also come up because of thoughts, daydreams, night dreams, or flashbacks. For example, "Today my boss criticized my work. It made me feel scared and angry."

Putting your inner experiences on paper may help to give you some distance from them so that you can better understand how and why you react to situations the way you do. Writing down your feelings gives you something to do with them so that you don't just obsess about them, deny them, or act them out. Most important, writing can also help you become used to identifying and labeling your feelings. As you become more comfortable with your feelings in general, you will also find it easier to communicate them to others.

When You Experience Dreams or Flashbacks: Use the Dream Journal

Keep another notebook by your bed and use it to record your dreams. As soon as you wake up write down everything you can remember, even if it doesn't make any sense.

Dreams may be difficult to interpret, since their messages are often cryptic and hidden. A simple rule of thumb is that every character, object, and event in the dream says something about you personally, because it is coming from your unconscious. You need not always take the dream literally (though sometimes this is the case); the messages need to be decoded through interpretation. It is also useful to attempt to tie your dream to something happening in your current life.

Next, write out all of your associations to each part of the dream. If you dream about not being able to swim, sinking under water and seeing the deep blue color, write down all your personal associations to water, not being able to swim, sinking, and the color blue. Tie those associations to what is going on inside of you. If your association to the color blue was sadness, you may find that you are feeling sad. You may be feeling overwhelmed by the force of the water (your feelings) and frustrated in not being able to swim (fighting them will only make them more persistent). Finally you ask yourself, What is this dream trying to tell me? Dreams are often compensatory; that is, they attempt to balance our conscious attitudes. If you've been avoiding your sad feelings, this dream could be telling you that it may be healthy for you not fight the forces of nature and by letting go you will naturally float to the top and not be overwhelmed by them.*

*For a more thorough description of how to interpret your dreams see Robert Johnson, *Innerwork: Using dreams and active imagination for personal growth* (San Francisco: Harper & Row, 1986).

John had started individual therapy after completing an inpatient drug and alcohol program. Thirty-nine, married, with a sixteen-year-old son, physically fit and owning a successful dental practice, he felt on top of the world. Yet he needed to better understand how he developed his alcohol problem in the first place—neither one of his parents drank. During the course of treatment he disclosed, for the first time to anyone, that he had been sexually abused by his uncle. Speaking of the abuse was painful for John. I spent several sessions just helping him get through the initial wave of intense emotion. After his revelation he came into session with the following dream.

I was in this old hotel where drug pushers and prostitutes hang out. All of a sudden there was an earthquake. The building collapsed and I was left standing alone. I was terrified, I didn't have a structure to protect me from the earthquake. There was smoke everywhere and dust in the air from all the fallen buildings. I couldn't see where to go.

John's dream was saying something about how he felt at the time of the disclosure. He felt as if he had been been in an earthquake. A sudden and potentially dangerous shift occurred in the ground on which he was standing. Facing the fact of his abuse had left him feeling insecure, uncertain, unsteady. In his dream he says that he was terrified. Yet he was unharmed. John, in spite of his emotional condition, was still standing with both feet on the ground. He was keeping himself together. In the dream there was smoke (where there's smoke, there's fire) indicating that he has some fires to confront. The fires could be heat, passion, or emotion that he needs to recognize and contain. The dust hadn't settled yet so it wasn't clear what direction to go. This was also true for John. He had just acknowledged his experience as a child. He was still confused. It wasn't clear what would happen next. I suggested to him that sometimes it's better just to let the dust settle, that is, let his emotions simmer off before moving on. This was a positive dream for John because we were able to talk about the process of healing.

As with dreams, writing down your flashbacks gives them room for expression so that they don't stay stuck inside of your head. Flashbacks can also give you valuable information about the nature of the abuse you experienced. Writing down in your feelings log the feelings that may arise from flashbacks will defuse them so that you can go about with your daily business and not be taken off track.

If You Can't Put It in Words: Use Other Creative Mediums

Some men have a great deal of difficulty articulating their thoughts and feelings. If this is so for you, you may want to sketch your thoughts, feelings, dreams, and flashbacks in pen, pencil, chalk, or crayon. Working in clay or wood, playing a musical instrument, or body movement can also help you to express feelings. You need not be "talented" in any of these areas to experience them. The purpose of these exercises is to release your feelings and thoughts by putting them into another form. No matter what medium you choose the process of acknowledging your thoughts, feelings, dreams, and flashbacks is a way to honor yourself and invite healing.

To Calm Yourself Down: Use Meditation

Sitting quietly with yourself and thinking peaceful, relaxing thoughts—or not thinking at all—can be quite an effective way of getting through the difficult periods of healing. Learning to quiet and soothe yourself is important simply because there will be times when you will need immediate calming down from your intense emotions.

Find a quiet place where you are not likely to be disturbed by telephone, children, partner, television, roommates, and so on. Get into a comfortable position and take a deep breath. You can close your eyes if you like. Take several deep breaths and, as you exhale, let your body relax. Focus on each part of your body one at a time (head, arms, chest, legs, and so on), and as you breathe out let all the tension leave that part of your body. Take your time. If all the tension doesn't go away the first time, don't worry. Like most skills, meditation takes time and practice. Once you have completely relaxed your body, or relaxed as much as you can, focus on a peaceful image in your mind (such as lying out on the warm sand by the beach), an actual object (such as a fish swimming in an aquarium), or just let your mind go blank. The purpose of this exercise is to relax both mind and body. If thoughts begin to intrude, just wipe your mind clean like an eraser on a blackboard.

When You Don't Know What Else to Do: Wait

An important part of the healing process is learning to wait out the storms of emotion or anxiety. Men are notorious for wanting to act on their feelings to make them go away sooner. Sometimes doing something is the right thing to do, but at other times it is best simply to do nothing but feel your feelings. You can learn a lot about yourself by doing this. You may learn that your feelings come and go on their own. You will learn that you *can* survive these intense moments of emotionality, confusion, or anxiety. You may even learn more about your feelings by experiencing them intensely.

If you are feeling overwhelmed, just quietly focus on your thoughts and feelings. Write down what comes to mind during the next couple of days. Use meditation if the feelings get overwhelming. Wait. When you are ready to act, you will know what to do.

If You Need Support: Talk with a Friend, Lover, or Family Member

If you are comfortable with the idea, consider talking with someone about your thoughts and feelings. You don't have to give that person details, but you may want to let him or her know what you are doing. For example:

- I'm reading this book on healing from childhood abuse and I am feeling very frightened (angry, sad, and so on).

- I'm reading this book on adults who were abused as children and I'm confused as to whether or not I was abused.

- I'm reading this book about child abuse and it's really painful to read.

Warning: Talking about your abusive experiences with another person, no matter how supportive and caring they are, can lead to a fight. How does this happen? When you begin to disclose the abuse you are likely to feel a little apprehensive about their reaction. Anger is likely to surface and you may become somewhat defensive. This is especially true if you don't get the kind of reaction that you wanted. If an argument begins to develop, take a break, cool off, and then resume the conversation. The last thing you want is to dump a load of anger onto someone from whom you want support.

If you find yourself beginning to get defensive or angry again, you may want to stop the discussion and find a counselor who can help you in this process. Chapter 4 suggests some specific ways to go about choosing the right person to talk with.

If You Want Support from Other Wounded Men: Join a Men's Group

If there is no one to whom you can talk about this issue, you may want to consider joining a support group for men who were abused as children. Meeting with other men who are going through a similar journey can be very supportive. It can be very reassuring to know that you are not the only man struggling with this issue.

For years I thought that I could deal with my past by myself. I never told anyone that I was sexually abused by my uncle, not even my wife. I figured if I could just forget about it, I would be okay. But the more I tried to forget, the more it would intrude in my mind. I would think about it during sex with my wife, even when I would affectionately touch my son.

Three years before my uncle died, my wife and I decided to let him live in our carriage house. Uncle Richard and my son were very close. I didn't think he would ever do anything to him. I would tell myself that he was too old. I didn't want to make waves between my uncle and my wife.

When my son was sixteen he was hospitalized for a serious drug problem. He told his therapist that he had been sexually abused by my uncle. Maybe if I had only been willing to talk about it with someone, he never would have done this to my son.

At least my child is now talking about it with us. I am now talking about it with others as well.

Throughout the book suggestions are highlighted (in boxes) with regard to counseling as an aid in the healing process. Individual, group, and peer counseling can make the healing process that much easier and quicker, and I recommend it to all men. This is especially true if you are having any of the difficulties described earlier in this chapter. If you think that counseling can help you in your healing journey, you may want to begin to look for support now. You will also find the names, addresses, and phone numbers of organizations that provide support for adults abused as children in Appendix III. Call to find what resources are available in your community.

Take Your Time

It can be very frightening to confront your wounds so directly and deliberately. Proceed at a pace that is comfortable for you. Don't try to live up to some self-imposed schedule. You cannot go faster than you are psychologically prepared to do.

Remember, there will be times in your healing process that you will feel very uncomfortable. Doing any one or a number of the previous suggestions will help decrease your discomfort but may not take it away altogether. It is important that you learn how to ride through the difficult times. You can do this by reminding yourself this is a part of the healing process. Try reassuring yourself: "I will get through this storm of emotion. I have survived this long and I will survive again." Don't forget, as a child you were able to survive because you could tap into an inner strength. This was the hero within you. Survival is not accidental or coincidental. It occurs because you have the hope that a better life is possible. You especially need inspiration when times are hard. Sometimes the optimism of the child is necessary for adults caught up in their hopelessness and cynicism. That optimistic child still exists within you. Make room for him.

Ultimately you need to believe in yourself and in your ability to heal. Use this opportunity to grow, to become happier than you have ever imagined you could feel. This journey is an adventure into unknown territory. The path will not always be easy. At times you will feel like turning back, but if you keep struggling, your efforts will be well rewarded. The adage No pain, no gain contains more than a kernel of truth. So use your failures, mistakes, or setbacks as opportunities to grow, to learn more about yourself and others. But be aware that, when happy, we are often content to stay that way. We want to capture those moments and never let them end. However, emotional pain is not unlike physical pain; it is our mind's (as opposed to our body's) way of telling us that something is in need of fixing and we need to pay attention to ourselves. Remember, emotional problems don't go away by themselves; if not treated thoroughly they may go "subterranean" and then resurface in a more virulent form. And they keep coming back until they are finally healed.

Finally, the healing process means rising above the childhood abuse and finding the many positive qualities in yourself that you developed because of—and in spite of—those experiences. For example, the abuse may have made you more sensitive to pain and suffering in others. Or, despite your conditioning, you may have made a vow never to abuse your child. In order to do this you will need to learn how to focus on your positive qualities as well as your problems. All along this journey you will get to know yourself better. You will better understand your reactions to other people and situations. You will also discover that you have choices in how you will respond. The rewards for your work will be higher self-esteem and, subsequently, more positive friendships and intimate relationships.

Knowing When You Are on the Right Track

Sometimes your healing process will be overwhelming, and confusion can set in. At these times it is important to keep things in perspective. You can't do everything at once. You need to slow down and trust that when you are ready to work on a particular issue you will take that step.

Throughout this book you will read about issues that need to be addressed so that healing can occur. It will be helpful for you to identify guideposts or milestones that indicate that the healing process is progressing and that you are indeed on the right track. Some of these guideposts are listed below. When you find yourself doing any of the following behaviors or accepting these attitudes you will know that you are healing your wounds and that you do indeed have the courage to change the things within you that are in your control.

- When you acknowledge that you were an abused child, you are on the right track.
- When you are able to ask for help from others, you are on the right track.
- When you acknowledge that you are no longer a victim, you are on the right track.
- When you don't blame others and take responsibility for yourself, you are on the right track.
- When you begin to show your feelings more, you are on the right track.

- When you are stopping your own abusive behaviors, you are on the right track.
- When you are not trying to control others, you are on the right track.
- When you are willing to take responsibility for your own abusive behaviors, you are on the right track.
- When you are willing to acknowledge the hurt you have caused others, you are on the right track.
- When you are being honest with people close to you on a daily basis, you are on the right track.
- When you are willing to recognize your mistakes, you are on the right track.
- When you are willing to help other wounded men, you are on the right track.
- When you are able to identify ways that you contributed to a conflict in your relationship, you are on the right track.
- When you are able to tell yourself that you are a good and valuable person, you are on the right track.
- When you are able to appreciate your partner's point of view, you are on the right tack.
- When you are able to tell your partner, "You're right," you are on the right track.
- When you are able not to let your old feelings and attitudes dictate how you will relate to others, you are on the right track.
- By reading this book, you are on the right track.

Chapter 3

THE ABUSE AND THE WOUNDS

If you are like most wounded men, you may not be certain if you were abused or if what you experienced was really abuse. Having a definition of abuse is a necessary first step to being able to say to yourself or others, "I was abused." Understanding how abuse affects men will also help you identify your own particular wounds.

What Is Abuse?

Think for a moment about what you consider to be abuse. If you are like most men, your first thoughts will be about physical violence—being beaten, having bones broken, being caused to bleed, or having been bruised. But do you consider fondling or oral sex as abuse? How about witnessing family violence? What about being called derogatory names or being locked in a closet? Most men don't immediately associate these behaviors with abuse. Yet abuse encompasses a wide range of behaviors and is not limited to physical abuse or violence that causes injuries.

The four types of child abuse are: physical; sexual; psychological (which includes witnessing spouse abuse); and physical and emotional neglect. These are not distinct categories; there is much overlap. In fact, children rarely experience only one type of abuse. For example, you probably also experienced psychological abuse if you were physically or sexually abused. Or you may have experienced both physical and sexual abuse. If you witnessed your father physically abuse your mother (psychological abuse), you may also have been a victim of physical abuse by either parent.

What do all these forms of abuse have in common? First, each form of abuse has a negative impact on the child's physical and emotional development. Years of professional experience have shown that one out of three adults who grew up in a violent home will experience serious problems. Second, all forms of abuse can be stopped. Both perpetrators and victims can break the cycle by getting help. This may be an important part of your healing process. You may be abusing others or be in a position to stop an abuser from hurting someone else.

Third, all forms of abuse are against the law. Child abuse is now illegal in all states. Why? Children, because of their lack of intellectual, emotional, and physical maturity, are unable to protect themselves from adults. Adults have more power over children and therefore must be prevented if they exploit that power.

Let's look more specifically at the types of behaviors included in each form of child abuse.

Physical Abuse   As with any definition of violence, the extremes are easy to identify. A light slap on a child's bottom is probably not child abuse, but breaking a child's jaw definitely is. It is with the in-between cases that you are likely to have trouble separating abuse from what you may have thought was normal punishment. You can distinguish abuse from "normal" or "acceptable" corporal punishment by physical and emotional injuries.

Physical injuries may have occurred as a result of having been:

- slapped

- punched

- choked

- kicked

- bitten

- burned

- clawed

- scratched

- having your hair pulled

- being hit with a belt, stick, cane, pipe, whip, or any object

Injuries range from:

- receiving bruises

- black eyes

- welts on the skin

- being caused to bleed

- having bones broken

- being wounded with a knife or gun

By today's legal standards, physical child abuse is defined as any corporal punishment that either leaves marks or is potentially dangerous to the child.

Jerry came to see me to learn hypnosis. He was a professional football player and need to stop a chain-smoking habit. I asked him when were times he was likely to smoke more. He answered, "Whenever I visit my parents." When I asked why, Jerry recalled having been physically abused by his father:

> My dad was a physician. Everyone used to tell me what a great father I had. We lived in a small town in western Colorado, and he was the only doctor. In fact, he delivered many of my friends.
>
> But I used to dread his coming home at night. He'd slowly pound his feet up the steps to the front door. I used to count the steps. He'd come inside, close the windows, and pull all the shades. He'd look for me to find out what I had done wrong that day. As he was looking he'd pull off his belt and start calling for me. I'd hide under my bed, in my closet, or down in the basement, but he would always find me. He'd make me pull down my pants and underpants. Then he'd take that brown belt of his and begin to beat the living daylights out of me.
>
> My ass hurt for days when I would sit down. My mother would turn away; she'd pretend that nothing was happening. I couldn't cry when he beat me or else he'd hit me harder. I hated him for so long.

Not all victims of physical abuse experience physical injuries. For example, Michael came to counseling to deal with his anger—especially with his wife. Although he was only five feet, four inches tall, when he would get angry he became a giant of a guy. He never hit his wife but would yell and intimidate her. He was abused by his stepfather, but never once was there a physical injury:

> He would slap me in the face all the time. I mean really all the time. I remember one week when he slapped me on eight different occasions. I was terrified of him.
>
> Sometimes he'd slap me for breaking a rule; other times he would slap me for nothing. He would sometimes correct my homework and make me sit down next to him and make the corrections. If I didn't do it right, he'd slap me on the back of the head.

I never thought of this as abuse because he never made me bleed—except on one occasion—or it never left marks. But when you asked me how I felt about it rather than what I thought about it, well, it felt like abuse.

Sexual Abuse

Sexual child abuse is any kind of forced or exploitive sexual contact or attempted sexual contact between adults and a person under the age of eighteen. To exploit someone is to take advantage of greater power or status over another person. Obviously, your parents or other caretakers, schoolteachers, neighbors, a friend of the family, or a day-care worker, had greater power and status than you. You might have been forced into sexual actions or manipulated or tricked into touching someone or being touched.

Sexual touch can be obvious or subtle:

- being orally or anally penetrated

- being touched on the penis or buttocks

- being touched sexually on the legs, arms, back, or other parts of the body

Sexual abuse may also involve:

- being forced to watch a person expose himself or herself

- being tricked or forced into exposing yourself

- being exposed to pornography

Bret, thirty-five and a lab tech at a local hospital, was arrested for sexually abusing his stepdaughter. Once he entered a group for other incest offenders he disclosed that he had also been a victim of sexual abuse. He described how his father would trick him into performing sexual favors: "My father used to come into my room at night and want to play a game with me for money. He would hide a dollar bill in his clothes and I would have to find it. He used to hide it in his ass or wrapped around his penis. I would touch him and he would get an erection. Then he'd tell me what I would have to do for another dollar."

Leonard, a seven-foot-tall bus driver who played professional basketball until sustaining a serious knee injury, was sexually abused by his father. He described how he felt intruded upon sexually by his stepfather before he touched him: "He used to undress in front of me and barge into my room when I was getting ready for bed. Sometimes he'd come into the bathroom when I was taking a bath or a shower and stare at me. I could tell he was getting excited. It felt so uncomfortable, but I didn't know what to say at first. He never touched me until a year or so later."

Psychological Abuse

Psychological abuse is very difficult for men to define. Psychological abuse includes:

- name calling

- humiliation

- rejection

- putdowns

- being degraded

- being belittled

- being made to feel ashamed of oneself

- isolation

- being corrupted

- threats of abuse

- threats to kill

- witnessing marital violence

Tony endured years of mental cruelty, or emotional abuse, from his father. Ultimately this treatment caused him to have low self-esteem. He was very critical of himself and would get very defensive at even constructive feedback from his wife. His wife insisted that they get into couples counseling, and Tony reluctantly went along. A shy man by nature, Tony described how his father would mentally beat him down:

> When he would yell at me, it would be so loud that I couldn't even hear the dog bark or the phone ring. He would corner me and stand over me like a raging monster. He would call me every name in the book, and then he would threaten to beat me if I didn't repeat what he said. I would call myself all those names, and he would raise his fist at me if I forgot one. Afterward I would look in the mirror and I would see what he said to me. I really was what he said I was. I didn't think about hating him; all I could think about was what a piece of shit I was.

Isolation

Having been isolated for hours or days is also considered psychological abuse.

Jerry described his being sent to his room for days on end. Tony remembered being locked in a closet for hours. Other men I have talked with have described being chained to the bathroom sink or tied to their beds. This type of psychological abuse—confinement—can be especially frightening. It caused each man to think that, as a boy, he was alone in the world, that no one could help him, and that he had to endure his pain alone.

Being Corrupted

Having been corrupted is another type of psychological abuse. This includes having been exposed to very negative role models or not having had limits set on your problem behaviors.

Barry's father frequently came home drunk with prostitutes and made Barry watch them have sex in the living room. When Barry became a teenager his father would encourage him to participate in these activities.

Having been abandoned by his parents, Rob was raised by his alcoholic grandparents. As an adolescent his grandparents would encourage Rob to get drunk. On occasion he would visit his real mother and would watch her freebase cocaine or use needles with her friends. In fact, she also allowed Rob to use drugs and alcohol, which ultimately led to his developing a serious addiction of his own.

Threats   Many parents threaten children with physical punishment if they misbehave. An appropriate punishment, such as loss of privileges, can be an effective way of teaching a child the difference between proper and improper behavior. Being threatened with violence, however, can be a very damaging form of psychological abuse, especially when taken to extremes. Sam, for example, recalled how his father threatened to kill him and described explicitly how he would do it with his hunting knife. Mark's father told him he would "break every bone in his body." Rob's grandfather would become verbally abusive when drunk. On one occasion he threaten to strangle Rob with his belt.

Witnessing   Another form of psychological abuse is witnessing violence be-
Parental   tween your parents. Such experiences can be terrifying for a young
Violence   person to watch and can leave deep emotional scars. Barry recalls the night his mother murdered his father:

Arguments between Mother and Father were a common experience growing up in my household. But I had a feeling that night was going to be different. Father was in his usual alcoholic rage, swearing at Mom. Chairs and other pieces of furniture were being knocked around. The sounds of slaps and punches echoed in my head. My mother's voice gradually became hoarse from her screaming and crying. Then there was a loud scream and then—silence.

Mom walked out of the bedroom, where most of the fights took place, and passed out on the living-room couch. I looked into the bedroom and I saw my father on the floor. I thought at first he was asleep; he lay there so quiet and peaceful. Then I saw the pool of blood.

The next thing I remember, the police were all over the place, asking questions, taking photographs, carrying my father away in a plastic bag, and arresting her. I hated them both and I swore at that moment I would hate them forever.

Physical and Emotional Neglect

You may not be able to pinpoint specific acts of physical, sexual, or psychological violence that occurred in your childhood. For you it may not have been what your parents did to you, but what they didn't do. In other words, they may have neglected to provide essential care to you as a child. Certainly the kind of clothes you wore, the type and amount of food you ate, the number of toys you owned, and the places you traveled were dependent on your family's financial resources. However, your parents may have failed to provide you with such necessities regardless of their financial resources.

Physical neglect includes:

- not providing medical care, food, clothing, supervision or proper shelter for a child

Physical Neglect

Leonard's stepfather drank away his paychecks. As a result, the family was forced to live in an unheated, barren basement for most of his childhood. Rob's grandparents didn't provide proper medical care for him. For most of his childhood they were out drinking, so Rob and his younger sister were forced to find food and cook for themselves. He frequently cut school in order to take care of his younger sister. One year he missed half the school year. His grandmother's response to the school principal was, "He's seven years old. He can decide for himself."

Neglect may also have been in the form of lack of supervision. As a young child, Michael remembered being left alone in the house for days at a time, having to prepare his own meals, wash his own clothes, and walk himself to school. After his father and mother divorced, Michael lived with his mother. She was cold, distant, and generally unavailable.

Andrew was referred for counseling as a condition of parole. Having been recently released from jail he was making an effort to get his act together. He was attending AA and had found a steady job as a machinist. Counseling wasn't new to him—he was "talking to the man" as far back as he could remember. He described to me what at the time seemed to have been a free and easy childhood:

> I used to think that I couldn't have had an easier childhood. My parents didn't care what time I came home. They would let me use their alcohol and pot. I would be stoned or drunk during dinner and my father wouldn't know the difference. They didn't hassle me if I flunked a class or got a notice for cutting altogether. Yes, I had an easy life. Then the trouble started when my girlfriend got pregnant and I got busted for drugs in school. My parents did nothing. I kept getting into more trouble and they kept doing nothing. I kept asking for help by getting into more trouble and they kept doing nothing. By the time I was fourteen, I would get drunk at home in front of my parents. I got kicked out of high school and started stealing to get money for drugs. I was in and out of juvenile hall for most of my teens and then when I turned eighteen I started getting to know the adult system. I have served two three-year terms in jail.

Emotional Neglect

Emotional neglect may be the most difficult form of abuse for you to identify in your own childhood. It also may have the most damaging effects on your life.

Emotional neglect consists of:

- not having been loved

- not having received affection, empathy, and genuine caring

Most of us can say there were brief times when we felt that our parents didn't love, care about, or understand us. But emotional neglect is not just a fleeting feeling you get when you don't get your way. It is something that is pervasive, ongoing, and evident in certain observable behaviors.

Tony felt unloved by his father. His dad never showed any physical affection and never told Tony that he loved him. His father was cold, distant, and still is to this day. When Tony was five years old he asked his father if he loved him. His father replied, "Only when you are good." Michael frequently was verbally abused by his father, so he grew up assuming that his father didn't love him.

The extreme withholding of love and affection can be as traumatic to a child as physical violence. Barry's father continually told him, "I hate you. You are a worthless son of a bitch and no one is ever going to want you." Sam's mother got drunk and called him "an unlovable piece of shit." It is easy to see how an emotionally abused child may grow up to feel extremely inhibited—prevented from discussing his difficulties with friends and family members, believing that he must solve his problems alone.

Having an alcoholic or drug-addicted parent can also cause emotional neglect. If one or both of your parents were generally intoxicated or high, they were probably unable to provide you with proper supervision, attention, and love. Even if only one of your parents was addicted, chances are that your other parent was so absorbed with the problems of his or her spouse that no one was emotionally available for you. If you grew up in a single-parent family where there was alcoholism or other addictions, you probably ended up taking care of your parent rather than the reverse, as it should be.

Having had pathological role models as parents can also lead to emotional neglect. Rob's mother was involved in criminal activity. Rob was exposed to all types of seedy characters as a child. For him, experiencing the dark side of life was commonplace. It was just as frightening for Rob to be in his mother's house as it was to be on the street. Most of childhood, he felt alone and uncared for.

The Effects of Abuse

The effects of abuse generally fall into three categories: emotional, attitudinal, and behavioral. If you suffer from emotional effects of abuse, you will either experience overwhelming feelings or have trouble identifying them at all. Feeling-reactions include: anger, sadness, loneliness, hopelessness, fear, anxiety, and depression.

Intrusive thoughts or flashbacks are linked with emotional reactions because they usually carry with them a great deal of emotional charge. When an idea or something we see or hear reminds us either consciously or subconsciously of the traumatic event, it triggers an emotion or memories connected to the abuse.

Attitudinal reactions have to do with your attitudes toward yourself and others. Two common reactions to childhood abuse in this category are low self-esteem and distrust of self and others.

Finally, behavioral reactions are the outward manifestations of feelings and attitudes. These include destructive behaviors, such as violence and addictions, and issues relating to sexuality, such as sexual-orientation confusion, hypersexuality, or loss of sexual desire.

Emotional Reactions
Anger

Anger is one of the most common reactions to having been abused. The pain of being rejected by a trusted adult created a bundle of anger that you have kept in all these years. Eventually you will express those feelings either directly or indirectly. More often than not, you will misdirect it towards others.

Anger is a normal reaction to being abused. Ordinarily anger tells us that we are uncomfortable with a situation and motivates us to respond appropriately. Unfortunately, you were probably unable to express your anger directly to your abuser because it only increased the likelihood of more abuse. You may have also gotten the message from your abuser that getting angry was inappropriate, disrespectful, or just plain wrong. But the anger doesn't go away by itself: it sits and festers. And over time that anger turns into rage and gets harder to ignore.

If you feel uncomfortable with your anger, you will purposefully try to avoid situations that make you feel more anger. Gradually your goal becomes not to feel or show anything. This pattern may be so automatic for you that you lose touch with your feelings altogether.

Sam still feels a great deal of anger toward both his parents. He describes why:

My father would come home drunk just about every night. He'd ask my mother what I did wrong that day. She was so afraid of him, she would tell him something just to keep him off her back. I thought she was a weak bitch for sacrificing me for her own ass. He'd come into my room and wake me up. He'd start hitting me

---

Don't Judge Yourself

This description of the effects of abuse is an overview of the most common problems that most men experience. You may find that you can identify with some of these characteristics and not with others. Try not to be critical of yourself for having any particular problem. No judgment is intended in these descriptions.

We all have problems that are uncomfortable to face personally, let alone talk about with others. Taking a good, hard look at your problems can be an excellent opportunity for you to beat yourself up or blame your abuser or family for your difficulties, but neither of these reactions will be helpful to healing. Beating yourself up only makes you feel worse, and blaming others gives away the power you need to change your life. This is why I emphasize the importance of developing a positive attitude toward your healing journey. For example, thinking of your healing process as heroic can help you to reframe your struggles in a positive way. It takes a great deal of courage to face your demons. Few men take on this challenge unless they are confronted with a personal crisis. Even if you are not face to face with such a crisis in your life, use this opportunity to come to terms with your inner feelings, confront self-defeating attitudes, and change destructive behaviors. Doing so will enable you to meet the challenge of life's adventures ahead.

with anything that was nearby—a ruler, a piece of track from my train set. Once he started poking a pen into my butt. I tried not to cry so that I wouldn't give him the satisfaction of knowing he was hurting me. I was terrified even when I heard the car drive up into the garage. I hated him then, and I still hate his guts.

Other Emotions   In addition to anger you may also feel sad, lonely, and hopeless. Your inner sadness at being abused can sometimes be beyond words. Being unable to express your feelings, you probably felt a great deal of loneliness. You think, "No one knows how much I hurt inside." You may also have felt hopeless, that the abuse would ever stop. The physical pain would disappear after a matter of hours or days, but this emotional pain has lasted for years.

Feelings usually travel in groups—if you're feeling one you may also be feeling others. Some men find that they have to express their anger before they can get to those more vulnerable emotions.

Like anger, these feelings are probably not easy for you to express, but they are just as important to release. Why? Because many of the behavioral problems are in part caused by a lack of comfort with or an inability to communicate these feelings.

Fear   Fear is another emotion that you have felt for many years. As a child it kept you alert and focused on danger and probably saved you from being abused at times. Today that fear may not be so helpful. It may keep you from making intimate commitment to others. You may be overly suspicious of the people around you. This fear may also keep you from expressing your feelings. In a relationship your fears can lead to jealousy and distrust.

Depression   When you do not acknowledge and express your emotions in a healthy way, feelings of anxiety or depression can result. Depression can feel like a cloud hovering over you, day in and day out. You will lose interest or the ability to concentrate in most activities. You may have a significant gain or loss of weight, sleep problems, fatigue, feelings of worthlessness, or even thoughts of suicide. Anxiety, on the other hand, may lead to excessive worry about self or others, physical restlessness or nervousness, heart palpitations, sweating, stomach problems, and trouble falling asleep. Medication can help to lift depression or calm anxiety in the short run, but learning to handle your emotions will ultimately help you develop true inner control over your reactions to childhood abuse.

You may be experiencing flashbacks in the form of fantasies, intrusive thoughts and feelings, daydreams, or nightmares. These are caused by unresolved traumatic experiences that carry a heavy load of emotion. You may remember specific incidents of violence from your childhood when you find yourself in situations that remind you of your abuse. You may also remember specific incidents of abuse when you feel emotions that are similar to how you felt as a child. Sam graphically described one argument he had with his partner:

Flashbacks

> I was chasing her around the house, and when I passed by a large mirror we had in the hall, I stopped and looked at myself and all I could see was my father. I saw his scraggly beard and messy hair, I remembered his alcohol breath, his clenched fist and the hatred in his eyes. There he was, or was it just my imagination? My father had died fifteen years ago but I saw, at that moment, that he was still alive—inside of me. I vaguely heard my wife crying in the bedroom. When I came to my senses, I went to the door of the room and I told her I was leaving. I spent the night in a hotel.

Sam's flashbacks were very real and present. And, most important, the flashbacks interfered with their ability to handle the present situation appropriately.

Your flashbacks may not be in the form of memories but of feelings. You may remember not specific incidents but the feelings that went along with those incidents. Sam was unable to recall all of the violence between his father and mother, but he did remember his reactions to it. He remembers feeling so upset that he would run into his room and hide in the closet and stay there for hours. Thirty years later, whenever he and his wife argue, he experiences those same fears and the desire to run away. He still wants to hide in his closet. The feelings he experiences are just as real as they were thirty years ago.

Flashbacks do not mean that you are crazy. They do mean that certain memories carry with them an emotional charge and therefore become intrusive, asking for attention. When the memories are discussed and the feelings associated with the event are also discharged, flashbacks are less likely to occur. Jerry had disturbing fantasies for many years:

> I used to have these thoughts about killing people. I'm talking about people that I loved. These thoughts would come up especially when I was angry. When I started coming to therapy, I didn't want to talk about them because I thought you would think I was crazy. What's interesting is that when I started talking about the abuse and getting my anger out, those thoughts came up less often.

If you are unable to deal productively with your feelings, either about past experiences or current situations, those unexpressed emotions will find an outlet in either self-destructive behaviors or acting-out toward others. Feelings, like termites, are not always apparent, but if you look closely you'll find them just below the surface, bent on destruction.

Attitudinal Reactions to Abuse
Low Self-esteem

Low self-esteem, feeling bad about yourself, and shame are common effects of child abuse. You may have received messages, both subtle and direct, that you were worthless, bad, or crazy. Your parents may have been extremely critical, degrading, or humiliating, and eventually you began to believe these messages.

Having been blamed for the abuse is another reason men have a poor self-image. The abuser may have called you provocative or seductive. You may have believed that you could actually do something to stop the abuse toward yourself or others. Eventually you began to blame yourself for the abuser's problems: "If only I had been a better child."

Over time low self-esteem becomes generalized. It affects every part of your life—home, work, play, and friends. Men with low self-esteem often find themselves being taken advantage of by others. They have difficulty standing up for their beliefs. They feel depressed, hopeless, and self-critical. Most important, they lose a sense of who they are as they try to live up to others' expectations and in the process lose sight of their own feelings and needs.

You may have the type of low self-esteem that is direct; you will just come right out and talk about your stupidity or worthlessness. Or you may take an indirect route, by acting as mean and tough as you can. That way you get others to think that way about you and you can tell yourself, "You see, you *are* a piece of shit."

Now that you have decided to heal, it is time to let yourself off the hook. That involves saying to yourself, and believing, that you were not to blame for the abuse. It also means telling yourself that you are a valuable, good person. Reminding yourself of this fact and acting as if you believe it can be helpful in the healing journey.

Barry describes such a change in attitude within himself:

When I left home my father could no longer beat me. Then I began to beat me. I was always telling myself how worthless I was, that no one in their right mind would love me. I was always messing up my life. I blamed myself for everything, including my parents' anger and unhappiness. I was carrying quite a weight on my shoulders. These thoughts about myself showed themselves in every part of my life. I couldn't keep a job for more than a year or so. I was married three times. I was always getting into trouble with the law. I had a serious alcohol and drug problem. I would look at all of this and just keep reminding myself how fucked up I was. It wasn't until I started dealing with the feelings beneath all of these behaviors that I began to turn it around. The first step was to realize that the violence wasn't my fault and that I had to stop beating myself up or I would keep on a downward spiral.

Inability to Trust   Like low self-esteem, feeling distrustful of others can lead to many problems in relationships. Because the ones you trusted the most caused you great pain, you learned that the people who are closest to you will hurt you. If you can't trust your parents or other important adults who are there to care for you, who can you trust? It is easy to see how you may have come to this conclusion. Because of your experiences with abuse you may have learned to associate trust and closeness with pain and rejection. When this happens, you may find it very difficult to let a woman or man get close to you. Your extreme difficulty trusting people may lead you to become overly suspicious or even paranoid.

William was sexually and psychologically abused by his stepfather. He was in jail for physically assaulting his wife. During an interview to determine if he was motivated for treatment he described how distrust can lead a person to suspiciousness or paranoia:

> He would fuck me in my ass so hard that it would bleed. I would hurt so badly the next day that I'd cut school so my teachers and friends wouldn't see my discomfort with sitting all day. I thought it was all behind me until I got married. I never really trusted my wife. I was always expecting her to hurt me in some way. Sometimes she wouldn't be home when I called or she would be late coming home at night. I would give her the third degree. She had to explain every movement she made, otherwise I would go nuts. It got to the point that I would miss work to follow her around during the day. I was looking for trouble. I was obsessed with thinking that she was going to mess around. It was ironic that I was the one who ultimately had an affair.

Behavioral Reactions to Abuse
Being Abusive Toward Others

Becoming physically, sexually, or psychologically abusive toward others is one of the most common behavioral responses to childhood abuse. Men, in general, are prone to acting out their inner feelings when they lack the skills to express them; and you may have learned in childhood that violence was an effective means to an end. Your feelings may be so powerful that when you do react it's in an extreme manner. This pattern may be so frightening to you that you try to suppress the feelings as much as possible. So you put your emotions into a trunk and hide the trunk in the basement of your mind. However, these feelings do not go away; they affect you every day, exerting their influence in many negative ways.

The combination of unresolved feelings and poor communication skills is dangerous. When a highly charged situation arises you are likely to respond in an aggressive manner if you haven't learned how to manage those feelings. In addition, you are likely to let out *all* those old feelings at the same time. The recipients of your rage are bound to feel frightened by the extent of your anger. If they are feeling the least bit defensive or criticize you for your excessive anger, an escalation is inevitable. If you escalate your already intense feelings you are likely to resort to the most primal method of coping with stress—violence. Violence brings about an end to the conflict but only serves to push the one you love away and gives you more reasons to get down on yourself.

Many men who were abused as children end up abusing their own children. This may occur for the reason stated above or for another, psychologically more complex reason. Having been abused you probably felt quite powerless to do anything to stop your abuser. He or she may have threatened or tricked you, or it was simply too dangerous to resist, given your small size and relative weakness. That sense of powerlessness may have followed you into adulthood. You may still feel victimized by others, helpless to determine your own fate. It is true that victimizing someone who is less powerful than you, over whom you can have control, can make you feel more powerful. The obvious problem with this method of feeling more powerful is that it is at the expense of someone else's safety (and it is against the law). You may think of this as a reenactment of your own abuse, but this time you're in charge. There are other ways of feeling strong and in control without infringing on the rights and well-being of others, especially those whom you love and should be protecting.

Treatment for Violence

If you are perpetrating physical, sexual, or psychological violence toward family members or others, there are domestic-violence treatment groups in practically every major city and rural areas as well. For information on the programs in your area, you can look up Battered Person's Aid, Crisis Intervention Service, Child Abuse, or Child Sexual Abuse in the white and yellow pages of your phone book. Here you will find listings of the programs in your community for battered women, child abuse, or elder abuse. These programs are usually aware of the self-help or therapy groups specifically for men who are acting abusive toward others.

Many of the programs across the country for child physical abuse, sexual abuse, and spouse abuse use a very similar treatment approach. This is especially true for the programs that utilize groups as their main modality of treatment. Developing an ability to manage anger, conflict, and other intense feelings is an important element in addressing any form of family violence. Building self-esteem, examining sex-role attitudes, and learning communication skills are also necessary in learning how to control violence. Some sexual-abuse treatment programs utilize drug therapy and desensitization techniques to help men control their impulse to engage in sexual activities with children. Child-abuse treatment programs also help to educate offenders about normal child development and healthy parenting practices. Parent-child programs include a stimulation-and-enrichment component that helps parents learn how to interact adequately with their children. This may include verbal interactions as well as physical contact. The wounded man may need to learn about healthy touch and communication skills so as not to neglect his children's physical and emotional needs.

Abusing Drugs or Alcohol   Substance abuse is another way to avoid feeling your pain. If you get high, then you don't have to feel anything. If you subsequently get angry and violent, then you don't have to feel the sadness and fear. In today's society there is a great deal of permission for us to anesthetize ourselves to our pain and misery. Alcohol is the most easily accessible drug to this end. You can use it to take the edge off the day, to induce a highly euphoric state, or to knock yourself unconscious. Other drugs such as marijuana, cocaine, barbiturates, amphetamines, and prescription drugs are also effective ways to numb yourself to your emotional pain.

The problem with this method of coping with pain is that eventually the anesthetic wears off and you have to experience the pain. And the pain will always be there unless you do something about it.

Compulsions, or becoming preoccupied with externals—whether it's work, exercise, relationships, or sex —are another way to avoid internal feelings. As long as you are focused on what's happening out there, you are not going to pay much attention to what's happening inside.

Compulsive Behaviors

The price for these compulsions is very high. As long as you expect something or someone to take away your inner pain, you will never heal the underlying wound that's causing the pain. It's like ignoring the fact that your car needs new tires. Sooner or later you're going get a flat. This is the relationship between behavioral reactions to abuse and feeling reactions. You can only ignore the feelings so long. Eventually they come out, and it usually involves hurting yourself or others.

The greatest cost of compulsive behavior is the loss of yourself. When you become absorbed with whatever you are addicted to, you lose touch with your own feelings and thoughts. You become a stranger to yourself. This is called alienation. If you can't have a real relationship with yourself, you won't be able to have one with others. You become a lonely person, with only your compulsion to keep you warm at night.

John, who was sexually abused as a child, had a number of compulsions that kept him from facing his own inner pain and anger.

I got involved in work. Involved is an understatement. I got addicted to work. I became so obsessed with it that I would spend all of my free time doing work-related activities. I hardly spent any of my time with my family. In fact, my wife would encourage me. I think she knew I was running away from something and I think she was as frightened about those feelings as I was. All the while, I knew on some level I was running away from something. And I just couldn't put my finger on it. I would work at least twelve hours a day. I wouldn't even go home for dinner. I'd eat out, and off I would go, back to the office until early in the morning. Sometimes I would sleep there. I never got to spend time with my kids. They grew up without a father. I was a ghost in their life. I lost touch with my wife, and she eventually left me, but most of all I lost touch with myself.

Sexual-orientation Confusion

Questioning your sexual orientation is a common reaction to abuse, especially if you were sexually abused by a man. In fact you may already have asked yourself, Am I a homosexual? Research indicates that there is a link between childhood victimization of boys and homosexual activity later in life. This doesn't mean that an abused boy will become a homosexual, but he might experiment with homosexual activity. However, the relationship may not be cause and effect. Some boys may, for a variety of reasons, already be predisposed to homosexuality before being abused. Therefore they may be more likely to be at risk for homosexual child abuse. For some boys an early experience with a man may have contributed to a decision as an adult to engage in homosexual relationships. For some men the decision to engage in homosexual relationships may be independent of a childhood victimization.

Sexual life-styles, for the most part, are determined by both biology and our experience. We are all born sexual beings, and the choices we make, either consciously or unconsciously, to engage in heterosexual, homosexual, or bisexual relationships are based on many factors, including physiology, early childhood experiences, and sexual experimentation. Do not assume that homosexuality is necessarily a direct response to child sexual abuse. Sexual life-style choices are complex and therefore cannot be reduced to one event or factor.

Homosexuality was the topic of discussion one night at a group for wounded men. To everyone's surprise, each man had either had a homosexual experience or contemplated such an experience at least once. Research has also shown that this is not unusual. Over one-third of all men have either contemplated or actually had a homosexual experience. Just the same, this sexual confusion can be very frightening to you if you were sexually abused by another man or by a woman. You are probably feeling afraid of what other men and women would think of you if they knew you had this type of experience. Their judgments of you can be especially frightening if you are also conflicted about your own sexual orientation.

John was confused about his sexual orientation, especially when he moved into an area where homosexuality was more socially visible.

My uncle sexually abused me, and it always left a lingering thought in my mind that maybe I was gay. As a result I never had any close male friendships as I was growing up because I was afraid of any physical affection they might show toward me. I was also afraid of what people would think.

When I moved to California I was especially nervous because I wasn't always sure who was gay and who was straight. And I didn't want anyone to think I was gay, that's for sure. I remember when I joined this men's group sometime ago, it was the first time I had ever made close men friends. Well, out here everybody hugs everybody. It's considered normal. But not by me. When one of my friends used to hug me in public, I would get real embarrassed. What if people thought I was gay?

I began to talk about my fears of being homosexual when I got into counseling. A lot of my fears also had to do with my being abused by a man, but some of my fears also had to do with a bias against gays in general. Hearing that I wasn't the only sexual-abuse victim who felt this way helped. Once I was able to talk about those fears and sort out my sexual-abuse issues from personal bias, I wasn't so afraid of men, gay or straight. After a while I could even let myself be affectionate with another man. Now I just don't think about it so often. I just do what comes naturally.

Sexual Behavior Problems   Sexual problems, such as hypersexuality or lack of sexual desire, or specific sexual dysfunctions, such as impotence (inability to get or maintain an erection) or premature ejaculation (ejaculating before you want to) can also be a result of childhood abuse. Intense feelings that are repressed may affect sexual functioning. Loss of sexual desire can come about either from uncomfortable feelings during sex or from uncomfortable feelings, flashbacks, or negative associations that do not occur during sex but affect it. Hypersexuality, like most addictions, can also be a way of avoiding thoughts and feelings about childhood abuse.

Chapter 4

BREAKING DENIAL: "I WAS AN ABUSED CHILD."

As a child you were probably very resourceful in discovering ways to avoid being hurt and lessen the pain and confusion. If you were fortunate, you were able to find help or develop a supportive relationship with an adult or peer. If you were less fortunate, you may have become violent or used drugs or alcohol to numb the pain. You probably also learned to use minimization and denial to get through each day. These methods of coping may have helped in the short run, but over the long run they only cause more problems in your life. Breaking through your denial and accurately naming your experiences rather than minimizing them is what the first stage of healing—awareness and disclosure—is all about.

Minimization and Denial

When you were a child, you probably never talked about your abuse. Your parents may have told you explicitly not to talk about family problems. They may have also minimized and denied the abuse, giving you a subtle message to do the same. For example, your abuser may have told you that what was happening was normal and that other children have similar experiences. The abuser may also have given you the message that others would think badly of you if they knew or that you deserved the abuse and that telling others would only bring you shame.

Evan, a seventeen-year-old high school junior, was referred to me because of truancy and aggression with peers. After ten sessions he told me his mother was teaching him how to masturbate. He described in detail, showing no emotion, the sexual acts perpetrated by his mother for several years. He told me that he thought that all mothers taught their sons about sex through this means. When I asked him who told him this, he said, "My mother."

Abused children not only minimize and deny the abuse, they may deny their feeling as well. Sam described his childhood as "feeling-less, walking around like a zombie." He would frequently witness his father severely battering his mother. His father would also physically abuse him. One crisis after another didn't faze him until one day a seemingly minor problem opened the floodgates; he began to express feelings long forgotten.

A year ago when I first got into therapy I was asked how I felt about my wife leaving me. I didn't know what the hell that shrink was talking about. Six months later, my father died. When I went to his funeral, I didn't shed a tear. About four months later I was passed over for a promotion. No sweat. A couple of weeks later I was fixing the muffler on my car and I cut myself on a piece of metal. It bled quite heavily. All of a sudden, I began to cry and cry and cry. I couldn't stop the bleeding or my crying. I cried uncontrollably throughout that night and most of the next day. I cried fifty-two years of tears I couldn't hold back anymore.

Sam's minimization and denial begin in his childhood but continued into adulthood. Like many wounded men he denied the abuse because acknowledging it would involve getting in touch with a lot of painful feelings. Facing the reality and pain of the violence was so disturbing that blocking the incidents from his mind was the best way to avoid the discomfort.

You may also have trouble acknowledging your abuse because of difficulty reconciling your negative and positive feelings about your parents or the person who abused you. It's easier for you to block out of your mind one end of the continuum, usually the negative. Bret, who disclosed in therapy that he was sexually abused by his father, said of him, "He was the smartest man I knew as a child. Dad was great! He was perfect—well, except for this one problem. But I still admire him a lot." Bret talked dispassionately about the abuse, always making a point to remind me what a wonderful man his father was. The goal of the counseling was not to get Bret to hate his father but to acknowledge the abuse and his feelings of anger toward his father. His denial was beginning to get in his way: Bret hadn't talked with his father for twenty years. He had no male friends. He was extremely dependent on his wife to fill all his needs for friendship and intimacy, yet he had trouble communicating his feelings with his wife. He was very afraid of her anger and would react very defensively. And now he was being accused of sexually abusing his stepdaughter. All of the problems in his life were forcing him to address this unresolved issue.

You may be prone to more denial and minimization if the abuse you experienced was not blatant. Andrew's father never hit him or screamed at him, but he never showed any demonstrable signs of love either: no hugs, no saying "I love you," no touching. He was cold and distant; no one was allowed to show feelings or to laugh. Evan's mother would walk around the house naked. She would sit down by Evan's side he was watching television, and begin to massage his body. Evan would feel very uncomfortable but couldn't escape. It was easy to say his mother was just trying to be affectionate.

How Do You Rationalize
Your Abusive Experiences?

Look at the list below. Which ones apply to you? What other rationalizations have you used?

Physical and Psychological abuse

- I was a difficult kid to raise
- I never used to listen to my parents
- I didn't try to stop them
- It was just normal punishment
- They worked hard and were stressed out a lot
- They would beat me only when I gave them a good reason
- I asked for it
- They were just trying to bring me up right
- It taught me the difference between right and wrong
- It made me stronger
- I fought back
- I was a dumb kid
- They had problems of their own
- They had too many children
- I was a demanding child
- I had a lot of problems
- I was always sick
- I never told anyone

Rationalizations   One of the most common forms of denial is rationalization. This comes naturally to men because we often believe that we can think ourselves into or out of anything. In this case we try to think ourselves out of feeling and remembering the abuse. We try to think ourselves into feeling good about our abuser or believing that the abuse was no big deal. But was it?

Neglect

- My parents had it rough
- They had too many children
- I was a demanding child
- They were just doing what other parents did
- My demands for love were just too great
- I was a sickly child
- We were poor

Sexual abuse

- I was seductive
- I didn't stop it
- I liked how it felt sometimes
- They needed my love and understanding
- I was too affectionate
- I wanted too much attention
- I would dress improperly
- My body developed too early
- I would encourage him/her
- I was lonely
- I was needy
- I enjoyed it
- He/she was lonely

How many times have you told yourself that you deserved to get punished sometimes or that you were a difficult child? These are called rationalizations, and we use them to minimize or deny abusive experiences. Evan would rationalize, "I was a very seductive kid. I guess my mother had a difficult time controlling herself around me." Rationalizations are forms of denial that serve to keep our defenses strong. Through rationalizations you can avoid labeling yourself as having been abused. Doing so keeps you in your head and out of your feelings. Ultimately this form of denial keeps the blame on yourself rather than on the person who perpetrated the abusive behaviors.

Rationalizations are often meant to excuse the offender because, after all, "They didn't know what they were doing." Bret's father was an alcoholic. "He would get drunk and lose control. He didn't know what he was doing. If he did, I guess he wouldn't have done it." Leonard understood his stepfather's sexual abuse of him as a result of his problematic marriage. "My mom was always with her friends. He was lonely and I was the only one around the house. I guess it was better that it was me than a stranger."

Your rationalizations are efforts to think away the problem, find an excuse for the perpetrator, or minimize the seriousness of the act. Most important, rationalizations keep you from feeling your emotions. But these feelings don't go away—and eventually they manifest themselves in negative attitudes about yourself or others and in destructive behaviors.

Rationalizations prevent you from ultimately healing your wounds. How do you break away from rationalizations? By acknowledging to yourself that it was abuse. You need to trust your gut. If it felt wrong, then you are right! Child specialists say that children have a built-in radar system that tells them when something is right and when it's wrong. If you can recall how it felt then, it might help you decide today.

Were You Abused?   Think about an incident that occurred to you as a child that you believe may have been abuse. Remember what led up to the incident, what the person(s) did to you, and how it felt at the time. Pay attention to your gut feelings. Knowing what you know now, do you think it was abuse?

It is important to say "I was abused," because labeling your experience as such means that you are willing to tell the truth. Abuse often happens behind a veil of secrecy. When you tell the secret you are likely to feel significant relief, as if you have laid down a burden you have been carrying for many years. Telling the truth is also necessary for you to acknowledge your hurt, anger, and pain. And doing so will allow you to begin to let go of those intense feelings you have been keeping inside for many years. Finally, as with any problem, it will be very easy for you to slip back into denial. Saying to yourself, I was abused as a child will help you to keep focused on your healing journey. This is not an excuse for you to feel sorry for yourself or a rationalization for problems. However, beginning to understand the root of your problems can help to change negative patterns in your life.

Disclosure: Telling Yourself, "I Was Abused"

The first important stage in the healing process is to break through your denial by admitting to yourself that you were abused. This may be very difficult because making this statement may contradict a deeply held belief that you were not a victim of abuse. Recognizing that you were abused may also mean viewing yourself, your parents, or the abuser in a different light. If the perpetrator was a family member, there may be a significant change in your relationship with that person. Telling yourself, I was abused, will also put you in touch with some strong emotions that may initially confuse you or make you very uncomfortable. As you break down some of your defenses you will become more vulnerable, less certain, less steady in your daily mood. Nevertheless, taking the first step, disclosure, is very important because this is where healing begins.

Can You Say the Words

Although you may have already acknowledged your abusive childhood to yourself, you may have never vocalized the words *I was abused*. Even if you think you have already acknowledged the abuse, you must say the words.

Find a comfortable place where you won't be disturbed and say to yourself, "I was abused as a child." You may want to be more specific and say, "I was sexually abused by my neighbor" or "I was physically abused by my father." Say it again. You may want to look in a mirror or talk into a tape recorder to see how you look or hear how it sounds.

How do you feel as you say these words? Are you feeling scared? Sad? Angry? Embarrassed? If you are having difficulty identifying your emotions, focus on your physical sensations. Are you tense in the stomach, chest, or head? Are you feeling light-headed or dizzy? If you are not aware of your feelings right now, that's okay. Identifying and expressing your feelings will follow as you develop specific skills in that area. If you have identified how you are feeling either emotionally or physically, say it out loud. For example:

- "I am feeling angry [or scared or . . .]."

- "I am feeling tense in my stomach right now."

- "I'm feeling very awkward being so direct about the abuse."

- "I don't know what I am feeling right now."

Verbally acknowledging the abuse and the feelings you may experience as you disclose the fact is an important first step in the healing process.

Remembering Details

Once you have admitted to yourself that you were abused, the next step is to acknowledge exactly what happened. This process will also help you better understand why the abuse occurred and how it ultimately affected you.

Many men have trouble remembering the details of abusive incidents. It is not uncommon to forget painful memories either consciously or unconsciously. However, remembering details can be important for several reasons. First, thinking about specific events will help you fight your tendency to deny the abuse altogether. Second, remembering details of violence helps you resist the urge to rationalize the abuse. Finally, recalling incidents of abuse helps you separate facts from fantasy.

Let's begin to get some of the facts down on paper. Think about one incident that stands out in your mind, that represents the kind of abuse that you experienced as a child. If you experienced several types of abuse by the same or different people, start with whichever type you feel affected you the most. Write it down in whatever way comes naturally. You may want to begin by describing the situation before the abuse occurred. Try to include your actions, other people who were involved, and your feelings. For example:

What Specifics Come to Mind?

> I was coming home from school one day with my report card. I saw my sister on the street, and she wanted to know how I did. I was scared to show her, but I did. She told me I was going to get into trouble with Mom because I got a number of low grades and check marks under behavior. I began to get really scared that I would get hit. I also began to worry about Dad's reaction.

Next describe as objectively as possible the abuse you experienced. This may be extremely difficult for you because of the feelings that it may stimulate, but try to get through this part of the exercise. The next stage will address how you feel about that experience now. Again, try to be as specific as possible in your description. For example:

> When I got home my mother wanted to see my card. When she looked at it I could see that she was going to explode. She began to call me names like stupid, idiot, lazy, and she said that I would never amount to anything. She went for the belt that was hanging in the kitchen and began to chase me to my room. I jumped on my bed and she began to whip me. She must have hit me twenty or thirty times. It seemed to last forever. I felt so scared and hurt. My bottom hurt for days after. I hated her so much. I remember wanting to run away forever. But I was stuck; there was no escape.

Your own memory is not the only source of information about the abuse. Talking with brothers, sisters, friends, and relatives can provide valuable information about what you were like as a child, statements you made at the time, and bruises they may have seen on your body. Some of them may have actually observed incidents of violence. Mark was able to talk directly with his family members. They confirmed some memories but not others, and they remembered incidents that he had long forgotten or thought were insignificant. Although initially Mark was very uncomfortable, his conversations with his parents and siblings about the abuse led him to feel much closer to his family than he ever had as a child. For them, trust is being rebuilt, and forgiveness is possible.

There may be evidence of your abuse in old keepsakes. Few boys keep diaries, but many girls do. Ask your sister if you think she documented incidents of violence from childhood. Drawings are another source. Tony, for example, was artistically inclined as a child. He would draw pictures that showed a very unhappy child. Some of his drawings were violent in nature and one in particular was a picture of his father standing on top of him with a club in his hand.

How Does It Feel to Read about Your Abuse?

Writing about these experiences is likely to bring up some uncomfortable feelings. If you can identify your feelings at this stage, try to write them down as you reread the last exercise. For example:

- "As I read about this incident with my father I feel angry [or sad or afraid].

- "As I read about the incident with my neighbor I feel embarrassed and ashamed."

You may also be feeling very confused and unable to sort out any specific emotion. If this is the case, simply identify physical sensations you feel right now. For example:

- "As I write this down I feel a knot in my stomach [or sweaty on the back of my neck or tense in my face]."

- "I don't know how I am feeling. I know I must be feeling a lot, but I just can't sort it all out at this moment."

As you begin to heal you are likely to feel many intense and frightening emotions. Over time you will be able to sort out the feelings and get better at identifying and communicating them. Don't give up; it gets easier over time.

At this point you may being saying to yourself, I don't feel anything when I think about the abuse. If that is the case, think about how you felt when you were a child. Try to remember your feelings at the time you were being abused. For example:

- "I felt angry at my neighbor for sexually abusing me."

- "I was really afraid of my father. I hated him when he'd hit me."

Remembering how you felt then may give you insight about how you are feeling now. If you can't remember how you were feeling then or now, try to imagine how your child, niece, or nephew (if you have one) would feel if they experienced a similar type of abuse. For example:

- "I would never hit my child the way my father hit me. He'd be afraid of me. I don't want that."

- "Sex with a child is wrong, just because it's wrong. My daughter would hate me if I did that to her."

- "I imagine a child would feel angry and afraid of his parent if he were beaten with a belt."

Cutting yourself off from your feelings is a common reaction to childhood abuse. This is particularly easy for men because our socialization encourages us to do this in general. If you can't get in touch with any feelings, don't despair. If they are within you, they will eventually come to the surface. Be patient.

Looking at the Effects Another important step in the healing process is to ask yourself, How are those experiences effecting my life today?" Disclosing the abuse and your feelings about it can relieve you of tension. Then you can begin to explore how to get beyond your intense feelings and change negative patterns of coping that have followed you into adulthood. John describes this process after a number of years of counseling:

> I used to think that my uncle had taught me about sex through his masturbating me. I never referred to it as abuse until one night. I was dating a woman who was the first person I let myself fall for since my marriage. Well, about six weeks into things she decides to go back with her last boyfriend. I was really destroyed. I felt so betrayed. I began to realize that the feeling was familiar. I couldn't figure it out. I went to a movie by myself and afterward I was feeling as anxious as ever. I called my brother and asked him if he would meet me after work. As I drove into town I began crying. I realized how angry I was at my uncle for betraying my trust. The experience with this woman reminded me of that hurt that I tried too hard to rationalize away. When I got to the bar, I met my brother. We walked into the back restaurant that was closed to the public and we sat down at a table. I told him I had been sexually abused by our uncle. The words just came out of my mouth. I had never said those words before. I will never forget his first words after I told him. He asked if I was okay. He was totally concerned about me. It felt so safe to tell him.
>
> He was the first person I admitted this to. What was so ironic was that he and I were just getting close. You see, he is a recovering alcoholic and he had stopped drinking about one month earlier. He was beginning to acknowledge that he was an alcoholic. I am so glad that I had him in my life at that moment. My healing has been slow but progressing ever since that night.

John never associated his sexual problems with his being sexually abused as a child. The betrayal he felt with the woman he was dating was so intense he began to wonder if his emotions were disproportionate to the event. He began to ask himself, Are these feeling coming from somewhere else? The thought of his uncle popped into his mind. It took him only a few seconds to realize that he really felt angry at and betrayed by his uncle. The words just came out of his mouth—"I was sexually abused." Even though he felt uncomfortable saying the words, his gut told him it was true. John had been in therapy for some time working on his marital problem in relationships, but the counseling took a different turn when he revealed to his therapist that he had been abused. The focus at first was to understand how his abuse affected him then and how it continued to plague his life as an adult. Gradually he became more aware of his patterns and worked on changing those that continued to give him problems in relationships with lovers, friends and family, work and school.

Men come to terms with their abuse for different reasons. It may be something that you read in a book or watched on television. It may be as a result of a divorce or during an intensely positive or negative sexual experience. A counselor, spouse, or friend may have brought the issue to your attention. In any case, a realization such as this is often shocking, frightening, and painful. But in most cases, the initial reaction is eventually followed by relief.

Telling Others

There is great value in discussing your experiences with someone with whom you have a trusting relationship. You probably often felt alone when you were being abused, but you don't have to feel alone in your recovery. When John first acknowledged that he was a victim of sexual abuse, he told his brother. Although he had many close friends and relatives, he instinctively chose his brother. Maybe it was because his brother had been in recovery for his alcoholism, and John intuitively knew that his brother would be particularly supportive and helpful.

Jerry had been in group counseling for one year when he

disclosed his physical abuse. His father had died the previous week. He had never told anyone that his father used to beat him regularly when he was a child. When he came to the group he dispassionately described the events surrounding his father's death. The other members were amazed that he showed so little emotion. After some prodding from several of the other group members, Jerry admitted that he was glad that his father was dead. With encouragement he began to express why he hated his father. He gave a number of reasons, such as "He didn't play baseball with me," that didn't seems to make sense. When confronted on this issue Jerry looked at the therapist and said, "He beat me." Jerry had never said those words to anyone before. He had never even said them to himself. After describing several incidents, Jerry began to cry. He cried for an hour and that wasn't enough. That night Jerry began the process of healing from those experiences.

Bret was at the movies with his wife, Leanne. In the film a father was inappropriately fondling a male child. Bret got up and left for a few minutes. When he returned Leanne asked him where he went and he told her that he went to have a cigarette. Although she had never seen Bret leave in the middle of a movie before, she decided not to say anything. On the way home Bret was extremely quiet. Although Leanne suspected that he was upset about something, she chose not to say anything until they got home. Bret didn't want to talk, but Leanne kept pushing. Bret complained about work, money, and all the other usual complaints, but Leanne knew there was something else. She asked if the scene with the father and boy disturbed him. Bret asked, "Why would it?" Leanne replied, "Because you have said that you thought your father did weird things to you when you were a child. I never asked before because I thought it wasn't my business, but did he have sex with you?" Bret stared at her. No one had ever said those words before so bluntly. He couldn't speak. He wanted to say something but the words didn't come out.

For several weeks afterward, Bret was unable to concentrate on work or home activities. All he could think about was how his

How Does the Abuse Affect You Today?

In Chapter 2 you read about the effects of abuse on children and adults. How did your own experiences with abuse effect you then and today? Effects can be feelings (anger, sadness, fear), attitudes ("I don't trust others" or "I like to be in control") or behaviors (sexual problems, aggression, substance abuse). Try to come up with at least one effect within each category. Once you have made your list, write down how you would like to see yourself change. For example:

- "I have a lot of anger as a result of my experiences."
- "I don't trust people."
- "I have a drinking problem."

- "I'd like to learn how to express my anger better and, hopefully, get beyond it."
- "I'd like to learn how to be more trusting."
- "I'd like to get help for my drinking problem."

During the Understanding phase of recovery you are likely to come face to face with unattrative parts of your personality. Remember, every man, wounded or not, has skeletons in his closet that he is fearful or embarrassed to face. However, coming to terms with these problems is how we grow and achieve greater levels of happiness and satisfaction. The road is rocky, but the final destination is worth the wait and the work.

father used to touch him in ways that felt good and bad. It was very confusing. Bret had known it was wrong, but he let him do it just the same. One night Bret came home from a particularly difficult day at work. He walked into the kitchen where Leanne was preparing dinner, and sat down at the table. She turned around and asked if he was all right. He asked her if he could see her therapist one time. He told her, "I think I was abused."

Through his therapy it was discovered that Bret had sexually abused Leanne's daughter. Although he was subsequently arrested and forced by the court to go to counseling, Bret made use of the circumstances to heal his own wounds.

Both of these men told someone else about their childhood abuse and that experience alone had a dramatic impact on their recovering from the effects. Who can you tell? This is an important question you need to ask yourself. When you choose a person, think about what you want from them. Do you want them simply to listen or do you want advice? You may want someone who will challenge you or push you to do something about your situation. Perhaps you just want to be held and supported. Take some time to decide what your needs are in disclosing the abuse. Knowing this will help you decide in whom you confide.

Whom Can You Tell? You may discover that you intuitively know whom to tell about the abuse. Maybe you will gravitate toward a lover, friend, or family member whom you can trust with this special knowledge. Perhaps you could only talk about it with a counselor or someone who has also gone through a similar experience. Think about all the possible people you could tell prior to making a decision.

Jerry decided to tell his spouse about his childhood abuse. He felt that she would be most supportive because she was, in his own words, "my best friend." Mark told his best male friend. Sam told his therapist, and John told his brother. Barry went directly to the person who abused him, his father, who denied it. Unfortunately, Evan told his father that he had been sexually abused by his mother. The father became hysterical and Evan ended up taking care of him by trying to calm him down and reassure him. Evan's needs were never met by his father. Michael also went directly to his father and confronted him right after admitting to his counselor that he was abused. The discussion quickly escalated into an argument and a physical fight.

Although the person who abused you could be a source of emotional support in your life now, I would recommend thinking twice before going to that person with your initial disclosure. There may be a time to talk with that person in the future, but it's better to wait until you have spent time deciding what you want to say and how you may deal with all the possible reactions.

After you decide whom you want to tell, it is important to decide what you want to say. It is not necessary to give details. You may only want to say, "My father physically abused me" or "My uncle sexually abused me." Details are not as important as just letting another person know that this happened, how you are feeling inside, and what you need help with. If you feel comfortable giving details, do so, but don't feel obligated if the person you are talking to wants to hear specifics. All you have to do is say, "I don't feel comfortable talking about specifics right now."

You may want to preface your disclosure by letting the person know what you want from them:

- "I want you to just listen and not respond."

- "I need your advice about what to do next."

The time and place is also a consideration. For example, you may not want to plan your disclosure when going out to eat in a restaurant or when there is little time to discuss reactions. It is important to be sensitive to the other person's needs. Michael wanted to talk with his spouse about being physically and psycho-logically abused by his father. It was late at night, his wife was exhausted after a full day's work, and she was coming down with the flu. Not only was it not the best time for her but, given her condition, he was not likely to get the support and attention that he needed. Find out from the other person when is a good time. Then sent the time and do it.

If You Have No One to Tell

If you are fortunate enough to have a spouse, lover, or close friend with whom you can discuss this issue, your healing process will move along that much easier. The process of healing your wounds within the context of an intimate relationship or close friendship can deepen the bond and increase communication and intimacy, but it cannot replace the additional benefit of personal counseling with a professional trained in the area of abuse or joining a support group for men abused as children. Therefore, you may want to consider joining a support group or seeing a professional counselor.

You may feel that asking for help is equivalent to acknowledging defeat. You may be thinking I should be able to do it on my own or What can a counselor or another person tell me that I don't already know? or Why see someone who is as fucked up as I am? or Only sick people go to counselors. These misconceptions will serve only to impede your healing journey. You shouldn't have to do it on your own. Asking for help is not only helpful but necessary. We can all stand to learn from someone who is objective and removed from our situation, especially if that person has traveled the same road.

Chapter 5

HEALING THROUGH FEELINGS

Facing painful inner feelings is one of the most difficult aspects of your healing process, yet doing so brings great rewards. Your first reward will be the relief of letting the pressure out. Later, learning to identify and communicate your feelings in a positive way will help to raise self-esteem and prevent destructive behaviors. It also means better communication and fewer arguments with your partner.

Getting in touch with your feelings does not mean that you should forget about your thinking skills altogether. In fact, a strong thinking function will help to calm you down when you're possessed by strong feelings. The key is balance, learning how to use both your thinking and feeling modes. You do this by first learning how to identify and communicate your feelings on a daily basis. Once you have this skill you can call on it when you think it's appropriate.

For example, one night Jerry began snapping at his wife and blaming her for all kinds of problems. This unusual behavior made him wonder if something was going on inside that he wasn't recognizing. He thought about it for a while and realized that he was angry about an incident that had occurred earlier at work. He apologized to his wife for snapping at her and started talking about his problem at work. She gave him support and even a suggestion or two on how to solve the problem with his boss. Jerry had to use his thinking skills to get to his feelings. Thinking helped him discover that he was not angry with his wife but was turning his anger at his boss to her. He knew that he needed to talk about his problem openly so that he wouldn't keep taking it out on his wife.

A week later, Jerry's thinking skills actually kept him from escalating an argument with his wife. She had come home in a nasty mood. He felt that she was attacking him unfairly, and he began to get really mad. Suddenly, however, he realized that she was acting just as he had the week before. Instead of reacting to her anger, he began to think, and he asked her if something had happened at work that she needed to talk about. That question stopped her dead in her tracks. When she started thinking about it, she realized that her day had been particularly difficult. If you work on balancing your feeling and thinking skills you will be able to call on either or both to respond to a situation.

Learning How to Hide Your Feelings

As a child, hiding your feelings protected you from the ever-present emotional pain or the actual physical pain of abuse. It was easier to deny your feelings than to face being rejected or criticized for them.

Although you are probably not consciously repressing your feelings today, the old habit might have become automatic. Even so, it can take quite a bit of energy to keep your feelings in check.

Bret was sexually abused by his stepfather from ages seven

through thirteen. At times the abuse was so physically painful that he learned how to escape his body through using his imagination. He would fantasize about flying high above his home and community, where no one could reach him. Today he still has trouble remembering incidents of abuse because mentally he wasn't there. When Bret became an adult, his fantasy world did not end. In fact, the pressures of marriage, children, and work led him to withdraw further from everyone around him. He habitually lied to everyone with whom he was close. He was extremely cold and withdrawn from his family. His sexual relationship with his wife was practically nonexistent, and he had frequent affairs with women he didn't know. His whole world began to cave in when his wife left him for another man. In his second marriage he was arrested for sexually molesting his stepdaughter.

Michael, a juvenile probation officer, realized through his work that he had been physically and psychologically abused by his father. As a child he quickly learned that if he showed any feelings he would get hit longer and harder. His dad used to yell at him, "Stop crying, you sissy. Take it like a man!" Michael is in treatment for alcoholism and spouse abuse. He never shows his feelings. If he can't solve a problem intellectually, it's not worth solving. His wife, in contrast, is very expressive of her feelings. They get into numerous arguments because when she expresses herself, he feels under attack, defensive, and at times explodes in a fit of anger—just as he was taught by his father. When he couldn't reason with his wife, he would avoid coming home altogether.

Rob, a forty-year-old lawyer, was psychologically abused by both his mother and grandparents, who raised him. He learned that if he was compliant and didn't ask them for anything, he could sometimes avoid having to deal with them. Rob learned early that the more agreeable he became the less flack he'd get from others. Rob was known to friends and coworkers as a hard worker. He could always be counted on when extra work needed to be done. He would never say no. At home he was the epitome of the good husband: he was always fixing this or that, he cooked, cleaned, and took care of the kids. He was so responsible he would even clean up other people's messes at work and at home. He was constantly letting himself be taken advantage of by others. Although he appeared content on the outside, something was eating away at him from the inside. He had numerous physical ailments—the only way he was able to complain—and he was a workaholic who made no time to relax or do the things that he enjoyed. Because he wouldn't burden his wife with his problems he felt alone in the world. Stress caused his body to deteriorate, and he had his first heart attack when he was only thirty-six.

Bret, Michael, and Rob have all carried with them into adulthood coping strategies that they developed as children to control or accommodate the abuse they experienced. Each man developed "feeling-avoidance" patterns early on that resulted in similar patterns as adults. Ask yourself if you do any of the following:

- Do you think away your feelings?

- Do you drink away your feelings?

- Do you get high to avoid feelings?

- Do you use fantasy to avoid feelings?

- Are you numb to your feelings?

- Do you have trouble knowing how you are feeling?

- Do you have sex to avoid feelings?

- Do you work to avoid feelings?

- Do you rationalize your feelings?

- Do you never spend time alone to avoid feelings?

- Do you avoid intimate relationships to avoid feeling?

If you don't deal with your repressed or avoided feelings, both those leftover from your childhood and those that occur today, you will be more likely to experience the long-term effects of childhood abuse.

Write down ten ways in which you avoid your feelings. Try to be as specific as possible. Note how each way actually helps you to avoid dealing with your feelings. For example:

How Do You Avoid Your Feelings?

- I drink to avoid my feelings. It's easier to just zone out after having a few beers.

- I think to avoid my feelings. If I think them away they don't bother me as much.

- I work to avoid my feelings. I'm so busy I don't have time to think about them.

Confronting your feelings is an important aspect of all four stages of healing: awareness, understanding, education, and transformation. First, it is important to become aware of and communicate all feelings. It is also crucial that you understand how your feeling-avoidance patterns grew out of necessary childhood survival skills. Once you are able to identify the particular ways in which you avoid your feelings, you will be able to recognize them more quickly and ultimately change them through learning new communication skills.

Finally, in the process of changing these patterns, a transformation will occur. You will have a better balance in your life, and you will feel empowered because you will have more options as to how you will respond to situations. And, most important, you will be less emotionally restricted by your own past experiences.

However, in spite of the potentially positive benefits of accepting and working with your feelings, you may have difficulty understanding why it is important for you to change this pattern. Imagine that after a heavy rain you go downstairs to your basement and discover a few leaks. You grab the mop and clean up. But what if you discover a flood? You are likely to feel overwhelmed. If you could get away with it, you'd probably go back upstairs, close the door, and forget about the mess. Perhaps you might think, There's nothing down there of value and I never use the basement anyway. You could forget about the flood and hope that it would eventually go away. You wouldn't have to get your feet wet and begin the long, arduous task of cleaning up. If you were to actually leave the water in your basement, however, the damage to the house could be irreparable.

In the same way, ignoring your feelings can create damage in your life. A flood of feelings are in your basement and the door is locked shut. You don't need to go down there to get your job done. You don't even need to go there to find a partner and have a family.

So why go down? Why bother with all that work? Because if you don't deal with your feelings appropriately you are likely to take them out on others by becoming an abuser yourself. Going down in the basement—getting in touch with your feelings and communicating them—has helped many men heal from the pain of childhood abuse.

Identifying Your Feelings

Feelings are physical and psychological reactions to events that tell us how those events are effecting us. We use many words to describe how we feel: happy, sad, angry, afraid, lonely, hurt, content. Some words describe degrees of feelings. For example, *irritated* may mean just a little angry, and *outraged* very angry; *blue* may mean just a little sad, and *depressed* overwhelmingly sad.

Feelings are not simply an intellectual experience; they are something you feel in your body, such as the nervous stomach that accompanies fear or the tension in the chest and arms that signals anger. Part of learning to identify your feelings is to get more in touch with your physical sensations.

Label Your Physical Responses

The first step in learning to identify feelings is to label your physical responses to emotions. What are your physical responses to anger, sadness, happiness, fear?

What feelings do you associate with these physical sensations?

- tightness in the stomach, chest, head, neck, arms, or other body parts

- lightheadedness

- "butterflies" in the stomach

- hot or cold sensations

- heaving or light, rapid breathing

- heart pounding

Does tightness in your chest mean fear? Do butterflies in your stomach indicate anxiety? Your physical signs may differ according to the feeling you are experiencing. Get to know what they are saying to you.

The next step is to identify your behavioral responses to feelings. Do you get loud when you are angry or sulk when sad? Do you tend to to withdraw when you are frightened or get critical when you are feeling anxious? Your behavior signs may be obvious to subtle depending on the feeling and the intensity of that feeling.

Identify Your Behavioral Responses

Behavioral responses to anger, for example, include the following:

- sulking

- yelling

- withdrawal

- physical violence

- criticism

Tom would get a knot in his stomach when he was feeling anger. He also knew he was angry by the tightness in his chest and the hot sensation in his head. Behaviorally he would act cold and distant. Sometimes he would become critical and verbally abusive. "I never thought that it was okay to tell someone that I was angry. I figured they were going to think I was starting a fight or something. I especially hated to hurt someone's feelings with my anger. But it turned out that I would hurt them anyhow with my coldness and criticisms."

When you are not able to identify and communicate your feelings, you are expressing them anyway—but they are out of your control. When Tony was finally able to acknowledge that he had been physically abused as a child, he discovered a reservoir of anger. But he was so afraid of confronting raw emotion that he refused to recognize it. However, it began leaking out everywhere. He made hostile comments at work, he didn't follow through with his commitments, he constantly criticized his wife and children. Everyone felt and experienced his anger. But when friends asked Tony if he was angry, he would respond, "I'm feeling fine." For Tony to acknowledge his anger he also had to acknowledge the degree to which his experience had affected him and reexperience the old hurt and feelings of betrayal. Many years ago Tony had decided to "take it like a man" and not let it get the best of him. It wasn't until he realized that his fear of his feelings was getting the best of him that he was able to become less tense, more tolerant of others, and more comfortable with himself.

Wounded Men and Anger

Anger is a powerful emotion that you are likely to experience during your healing journey, yet you may become overwhelmed by the intensity of your feelings if you have a great deal of difficulty recognizing and communicating anger. In order to get more comfortable with your anger it's important to look at what it is, where it comes from, and why it is so helpful to recognize and communicate it to yourself and others.

What Is Anger?

Anger is an emotion that is usually provoked by an event, interaction, or thought. You can tell you are angry because it causes a physiological reaction. You *feel* anger; it is not just an intellectual experience.

Think about a time when you definitely felt angry. What sensations did you feel in your body? How did you behave?

Anger is a normal reaction to a grossly abnormal situation. It is a common reaction to being abused because abuse is a violation of trust and it causes a great deal of physical and emotional pain. But for many abused children expressing anger is simply not an option because doing so may cause more abuse and generate more anger. So they learn to avoid it at all costs.

Where Does Anger Come From?

You may be afraid of becoming violent if you get in touch with your anger. This fear may be justified if your experiences with expressing anger have been negative.

Much of what we intellectually know about anger, as well as other feelings, is learned—or not learned—in our families. So it may be helpful for you to look at how your family handled anger. This is Barry's story:

> One time I told my mother that I was mad at her, and she immediately slapped me in the face an sent me to my room. I wasn't allowed to tell them anything when it came to feelings. They weren't even interested. Whenever my dad would get mad he'd throw things about—including my mother—and we would all run for cover. So I learned two modes: Shut up and go to my room, or go nuts. That's what I have been doing all my life. I try to communicate my anger directly, but it's not natural to me. I still want to go to my room or kick ass. It reminds me of when I first stopped drinking. I was able to stop after a while, but the urge to anesthetize myself was strong and kept coming back for years.

Barry is right about comparing the urge to drink with the urge to resort to old patterns of coping with anger. However, we know that the longer a person stays sober the less urge these is to drink. Likewise, it you begin to change your pattern of dealing with anger, those old urges to hide away or act out will eventually become less strong. Through counseling Barry found a safe place where he could begin to express himself without getting punished or abused. Eventually he was able to express his anger outside the counseling office with his wife, his friends, and even with his family.

How Did Your Family Express Anger?

Think about the messages your father and mother gave you about expressing anger. Were these feelings ever discussed? Answer each question below.

- How did your father express anger? Give several examples.

- How did your mother express anger? Give several examples.

- How did your siblings express anger? Give several examples.

- Was it okay for you to express anger? If you weren't able to express it directly, what did you do with it?

Why Recognize and Communicate Anger?

Anger is a common emotion that all people feel at one time or another. It is not just a privilege of wounded men. When something upsets us we are likely to feel angry. Therefore, long after healing, you are bound to come across situations that cause you to feel angry. This is why it is important to learn how to recognize and communicate your feelings.

If we do not properly recognize and deal with anger it can lead to periodic abusive explosions, stress-related illnesses, and addictions. Think about it. Have there been times when your anger has seemed to come out of nowhere? Have you found your body developing aches and pains from holding anger in? Do you blow up at others? Do you feel good about the way you deal with anger? Do your family and friends feel good about the way you deal with anger?

Anger is likely to surface when you begin talking about your childhood abuse. At first it may be diffuse or generalized. You don't know who you're angry at or why, but you know that you are feeling it. Or it may be directed toward your abuser or other family members for not protecting you. During this time you should take the opportunity to learn how to deal with your anger in a positive and constructive manner.

Feeling pain is actually necessary for survival. When you have a physical problem your body responds so that your mind will take note: I need a doctor, or I need to lie down, or I need to take some medicine. Anger gets our attention in the same way. It tell us when someone is stepping on our toes either literally or symbolically, and its very presence demands a response: simple recognition, verbal response, physical fighting, or leaving the situation.

Anger Is Necessary

If we ignore anger it can intensify over time. Unresolved anger can lead to a variety of problems, from violence and chemical abuse to depression and hostility. Anger that goes unchecked is also stressful to your body and can cause physical problems such as ulcers, headaches, back pain, and a host of other ailments. In an intimate relationship repressed anger can cause emotional outbursts and emotional distance. Sexuality problems may also be related to repressed anger.

Why bother recognizing and expressing anger? Because whether you recognize it or not, anger is a part of everyday living. If you don't pay attention to it, it will continue to escalate.

Mark describes his anger habits:

I never used to get angry. Let me rephrase that. I never used to admit to myself, let alone to others, that I was feeling angry. I was angry all right, I would just let it out in indirect ways. I was sneaky. I was afraid that they wouldn't like me, or they would get angry back, or they would think I was out of control if I showed my anger. Of course my worst fear was that I would get out of control. I would show my anger in such hostile, indirect ways people were always pissed off at me anyway. When I learned to communicate my anger directly I felt better about myself and the person I was angry at. They also felt better about me.

You can ignore your anger, you can bury it, you can try to drink it away, you can blame others for it, you can try to rationalize it—but it always comes back. The point is not to repress anger altogether but to use it appropriately. This old Bengalese story illustrates the value of expressing anger:

On a path that went by a village, there lived a cobra who used to bite people on their way to worship at the temple there. As the incidents increased, everyone became fearful, and many refused to go to the temple. The swami who was the master at the temple was aware of the problem and took it upon himself to put an end to it. He used a mantra to call the snake to him and bring it into submission. The swami then told the snake that it was wrong to bite the people who walked along the path to worship and made him promise sincerely that he would never do it again.

Soon it happened that the snake was seen by a passerby upon the path and it made no move to bite him. Then it became known that the snake had somehow been made passive, and people grew unafraid. It was not long before the village boys were dragging the poor snake along behind them as they ran laughing here and there.

When the temple swami passed that way again he called the snake to see if he had kept his promise. The snake humbly and miserably approached the swami, who exclaimed, "You are bleeding. Tell me how this has come to be." The snake was near tears and blurted out that he had been abused ever since he had made his promise to the swami. "I told you not to bite," said the Swami, "but I did not tell you not to hiss.*

*An excellent discussion of this issue and this story can be found in Carol Tavris, *Anger: The misunderstood emotion* (New York: Touchstone, 1982).

Today's Anger, Yesterday's Anger, and Old Baggage

Anger comes in three packages: Today's, yesterday's, and old baggage. Today's anger relates to an immediate situation and is over and done with when the situation is resolved. Yesterday's anger is an accumulation of emotion—anger you have not expressed that explodes during a trigger situation. Old baggage is anger so heavy that it can break the toe of the person who gets in the way when you drop it on them.

Today Tom woke up late and had to rush to get to work on time. **Today's**
He got to his car and saw it had a flat tire. His wife said, "Good **Anger**
thing it's only flat on the bottom!" Tom wasn't in the mood to joke.
He was feeling angry. His stomach was in knots and he told himself
how pissed he was feeling. Once he changed the tire he was able to
calm himself down, and he didn't let it bother him the rest of the
day. He was even able to joke about it with coworkers later that
morning.

Barry's wife had been very busy at work for the past six months. She **Yesterday's**
felt that she had no time to relax and have fun with him or the kids. **Anger**
This was not the first time she had dropped out of the family
emotionally. Barry had always tried to be understanding and
supportive of her work, and that meant a lot to her. Recently,
however, he has been getting annoyed by her frequent absences. He
hasn't said anything, but the annoyances have been building up, and
now he is feeling angry. One morning as they were discussing
money—a topic that already carried a heavy charge—an argument
seemed to develop out of nowhere. She was telling him she needed
a vacation away from everyone and everything but didn't see how
they could afford it. All of a sudden he found himself yelling at her,
"You never seem to have any time for us anymore!" This anger was
an accumulation of anger from several situations that he did not
communicate.

Sam's father brutally beat his mother on numerous occasions. Sam **Old Baggage**
would often try to intervene, only to become a victim of his father's
rage. Both his mother and father were heavy disciplinarians. As an
adult Sam had tried to forget his childhood, and dismissed his
experiences as "water under the bridge." Sam's wife, Carol, was very
outgoing and expressive of her thoughts and feelings. She would try to
get Sam to talk about what was going on inside, but with no success.
The more she pushed him to talk, the more he would withdraw. Most
of the time she would just give up and leave him alone.
    One day Carol was expressing her concerns about the yard work

not getting done, and Sam became defensive. He slipped into his usual pattern and began to withdraw. This time, instead of retreating, Carol calmly persisted, and Sam felt backed into a corner. From deep down inside swelled up overwhelming feelings of rage and hatred. When she saw the look in his eyes she was afraid. Sam's old baggage, compounded with today's and yesterday's anger, came to the surface in an intimidating and possibly abusive manner.

Conflict, anger, and criticism are all very sensitive issues for Sam. Growing up in a family where anger was expressed violently left a strong impression on him. Whenever he encounters such situations today those old feelings flood his body, and it becomes difficult for him to think clearly. It is as if he becomes possessed.

Sorting Out Anger

If you are like most wounded men, you probably have a great deal of difficulty separating out the old baggage—that is, your anger as a result of the abuse—from yesterday's and today's anger. A good clue to when old baggage is being opened is when the amount of anger is more than the immediate situation calls for.

Once you are able to step back and realize that a good portion of the emotion you are feeling is old baggage unrelated to the current problem, your anger will immediately lessen in intensity. The other person will seem less threatening and may even be able to support you at that moment.

This concept may be very hard for you to grasp if you have never experienced this phenomenon. Essentially you are removing yourself from the intensity of the interaction for a moment and asking yourself: When have I felt this way before? Is this familiar? Is this old baggage? Barry and his wife, Louise, had a close encounter with old baggage one night on their way home from the movies.

We were driving home after seeing this lousy movie. Well, at least I thought it was lousy. Louise thought it was just great. Anyway, we were talking about what we liked and didn't like about it. I told her that I thought it was awful and she began to ask me why. Well, as I began to tell her my thoughts, she said I was wrong.

That she couldn't accept the basis of my feelings, whatever that meant. We began to raise our voices. I kept telling her why I didn't like the movie and she would tell me that my feelings were based on inaccurate assumptions or something like that. We came to a stoplight and at this point neither one of us was listening to the other person. All of a sudden I felt overwhelmed, and I just grabbed her by the blouse and shoved her into the door. She got out and walked the rest of the way home. The rage seemed to come out of nowhere. One second I was feeling tense, the next I was exploding.

This wasn't the first time Barry had exploded so violently, and the next morning Louise moved out to live with her parents. These events brought Barry into counseling several weeks later. Through counseling he learned about his anger, especially his old baggage resulting from being physically abused by his father. His father had always been very critical of him and had never allowed him to express his feelings, anger in particular. It took him quite a while to realize that although Louise's way of discussing the movie may have been disturbing, he did overreact. Once he was out of the situation he was able to see clearly the similarity between her response and his feeling about his father's abuse. As he learned how to express his anger more appropriately, he became better at recognizing when his old baggage was getting in his way of dealing with conflict situations. Several weeks ago he told me about a similar interaction with Louise, but this time he was able to step back a bit and catch a negative pattern before it took control:

The other morning when we woke up Louise wanted to talk about money. Can you believe it? First thing in the morning. But it was important to her and it was the only time we had together before we went about our daily schedules. She wanted to talk about starting a savings account for the children. She suggested putting one hundred dollars aside each month in an account. I suggested that we put our tax refund in the account instead, since we needed the extra money each month for bills. She quickly responded by saying that she'd rather get into the habit of saving each month. I started to feel like she didn't want to hear my ideas.

Well, I began to feel tense, and I raised my voice, accusing her of wanting to control our money decisions. The minute the words left my mouth I realized that I was overreacting to her suggestion. I got out of bed and sat at the foot of the bed and thought for a few seconds. She was pushing me to talk, but I didn't want to say another word. I knew if I did I would explode. After a few minutes I turned around and told her that this conversation was bringing up some feelings of anger. I also think that some of it doesn't have to do with her or our conversation. I told her that I needed a few minutes to calm down. She backed off and got up to get dressed. I did the same. As we were eating breakfast I told her that I was beginning to feel frustrated because I didn't think she wanted to hear my thoughts and feelings. I felt this way a lot as a child. I told her I needed to stop because I was afraid of overreacting. Interestingly enough, the time-out also gave her time to think about what was going on with her. She told me that she was beginning to experience old fears and anger as well. Her father would spend most of his paycheck on alcohol, drugs, and prostitutes, so her mother had to work to support the family. I guess Louise was afraid that if we didn't have a savings account the same would happen to our children. After this talk we were able to hug and come to a decision about our savings account.

Barry and Louise were able to step back before the conflict escalated and take a look at where their anger and defensiveness were coming from. Doing so immediately deescalated the conflict and eventually brought about a resolution. As an extra bonus they learned something new about each other and ultimately felt better about themselves.

It is equally important to separate yesterday's anger from today's anger. If you have been stuffing your feelings about something for the past several months, you are going to overreact when you reach your limit. This is why I encourage you to keep your anger account current: Don't let your anger accumulate. Here's how Michael and his family wipe the slate clean every month:

> Once a month we all get together after dinner and sit around and get old anger off our chests. The kids really get a kick out of it, but you know, it has really helped me and my wife. We not only get our angers toward each other off our chest, but we also keep current with the kids as well. If things get out of control, we call a time-out and everyone cools down for five minutes. Since we have initiated this ritual, we have found ourselves getting little angers out more frequently so that they never build up to big angers. We end our ritual with appreciations so that we don't just get focused on anger.

Use the anger-identification skills you have learned in this chapter to pinpoint yesterday's anger and old baggage. What are you physical sensations? What are the behavioral cues of your anger? Use your feeling log, described in Chapter 2, to become more familiar with your particular anger patterns. You can also use the other suggested exercises to cope constructively with intense periods of anger. Learning how to communicate your anger will help ease the pressure of the old baggage and decrease the likelihood of acting it out in destructive ways.

Communicating Anger

You can communicate your anger in many verbal and nonverbal ways. The possibilities are endless. Some ways, however, may actually lead to your feeling more anger, whereas others will help to dissipate the feeling. Stuffing, escalating, and directing are three ways people cope with their anger. You have probably used all three at various times in your life.

Stuffing

Stuffing is exactly what it sounds like. It is preventing anger from reaching the surface by keeping it stuffed inside.

Whenever we have something we don't want to show others, we

hide it. We may put it in the back of a closet, a drawer that no one is likely to look in, or that old trunk in the basement. Stuffing does work for a while. However, if you stuff your closet full of all your old possessions, one day the closet will reach its capacity and those items will fall on your head. In the same way, if you stuff your anger, one day it will spill out to batter you, your friends, and your family—whoever's standing in the way.

Stuffers hide their anger in different ways. Rob would withdraw and hide from whatever was making him angry, hiding even from himself. When asked directly if he was angry, he would say, "I'm not angry" or "I'm fine." A good stuffer will find all kinds of reasons to stuff his anger. For example, Tom would make up excuses for anyone with whom he might become angry:

> One night I was driving home from work and I saw my girlfriend, Donna, walking very affectionately with another man. As soon as I began to start feeling physically tense, my "Don't get angry" tapes went off in my head. They went something like this: Donna has been lonely lately because I've been working such long hours, and she really must get bored at home, and she doesn't really mean to get me jealous, and on and on and on. It was like I didn't have the right to get angry. So I never brought it up. I dropped it even though it ate me up inside.

Making up excuses can be one way of stuffing anger. When I asked John if he could get angry at his father he said, "I haven't had the time to talk about it with him. He's been sick a lot and it hasn't been the best for him." Doubting yourself is another way of stuffing anger. "Do I really have the right to get angry? It wasn't that bad." Thoughts of low self-esteem can also be a way of stuffing your anger. Have you ever told yourself that you were stupid or silly to feel angry about something that happened so long ago?

You can also talk yourself out of feeling angry by intellectualizing. For example, Mark was a very successful businessman because of his keen analytical skills. He had everyone figured out, including himself. When he would become angry he would try to analyze the other person to the point that he didn't have to feel his anger. There may be times when making the decision to stuff your anger is appropriate, such as when you are receiving a ticket from a police officer or when you are meeting your in-laws for the first time. But unless you deal with the feelings at a later time, you may be asking for trouble.

Stuffing your anger can be a problem for several reasons. First, there is the pressure-cooker effect. After stuffing for days, months, or years, you will reach a point when you can't hold it in any longer. This is when you are most vulnerable to an explosion. If you grew up in a violent home, violence could be part of that explosion. If you are from a home where alcohol or drugs were abused, you may use them to anesthetize yourself. Stuffing could also result in physical illness, such as ulcers or headaches. The more you stuff your anger the more your body and mind will experience stress. Stuffing can result in chronic tension, confusion, or even depression. It may also result in feeling alienated from others.

Do you stuff your anger in any of the following ways? Do you stuff your feelings in other ways?

- Denial: "I'm not angry."

- Sympathy: "She really doesn't mean to upset me."

- Low-self-esteem thoughts: "I'm stupid for feeling upset."

- Self-doubt: "Do I have a right to feel angry?"

- Intellectualizing: "I feel like they're just trying to push my buttons."

- Withdrawal: "I'm going to avoid that person."

- Excuses: " I haven't gotten around to it."

Escalation

Escalation is another way of dealing with anger. It's similar to stuffing in that you say or do things that are likely to make you feel more angry rather than less. But with escalation the buildup is much faster.

Sam and Carol were in my office less than one minute when the following argument developed. They were supposed to meet at a particular time and place to come to the appointment together. Apparently, they got their signals mixed and ended up driving separately. As a result Carol was fifteen minutes late for the appointment.

CAROL: What happened to you today? You were supposed to meet me at 4:30 in front of your office.

SAM: You don't know what you're talking about. You never told me about it. You always do this—you make plans and then you don't tell me about them. You really make me angry. You can be really stupid sometimes. Why do you do this?

CAROL: You're crazy. You're the one who . . .

It's clear where this discussion is leading. Both Sam and Carol seem to have their escalation techniques perfected.

Escalaters are easy to recognize because they being their sentences with "you." They don't talk about their own anger; instead they accuse others of wrongdoings. They may also ask provocative questions, such as, "Why did you do that?" Although they may not directly accuse the other person, there is usually an accusatory tone in the way they ask the question. Blaming is another common tactic used by the escalater to make the other person wrong. Why is it so important to make the other person wrong? Probably because the escalater doesn't like feeling his anger. When he does experience his feelings, he becomes very uncomfortable. Blaming the other person takes the heat off him and keeps the focus on the other person's shortcomings. Escalaters are also famous for calling names and swearing. You can see that both Carol and Sam were adept at that skill.

Escalation can lead to physical or psychological violence, which can leave emotional scars that may take many years to heal.

Usually nothing gets accomplished when you try to solve a problem with an escalater. Some escalaters make up as passionately as they tear down. Life with an escalater can be like a roller coaster, thrilling but exhausting. And, once again, problems never get solved.

Here are some ways we escalate our anger:

- by blaming

- by accusing others of wrongdoing

- by asking defensive or provocative questions

- by calling names

- by swearing

- by thinking paranoid or suspicious thoughts

- by making a case against someone before getting their side

Some of these patterns of dealing with anger may seem familiar to you. In fact, you have probably both stuffed and escalated at one time or another. You may believe there is no other way to deal with your anger, but there is: directing. Directing your anger is not always as immediately "gratifying" as withdrawing or exploding, but it can prevent many of the unwanted negative consequences you may experience with the other methods.

When you stuff your anger you deny feelings, saying "I'm fine." **Directing** When you escalate your anger you blame the other person, saying, "This is *your* fault!" When you direct your anger, you simply say to yourself or others, "I am feeling angry." Directing also means you must communicate your needs at the moment. Directing is not dramatic. Initially it may seem unnatural, contrived, and awkward, but with practice it will become second nature and its rewards will become apparent.

You will need to develop new skills, because directing involves talking. Stuffing, therefore, is not going to give you practice at directing. Directing doesn't involve putting others down or blaming them, so your escalation skills probably won't help you much either. Here's the formula for directing:

"I am feeling angry that _____ ."

"I would like _____."

How would Sam and Carol's conversation have gone had they used this formula?

CAROL: I'm feeling angry that you didn't meet me in front of your office as we agreed this morning. I would like us to be clear next week before we go to work or to talk with each other during the day to make plans.

SAM: OK. That sounds like a good idea. I also feel angry when I don't know about plans that you make. I would also like us to be more clear about our plans with each other.

When I encouraged Barry and Karen to try directing their anger, they remarked that it wasn't as exciting as their regular pattern of relating. They both agreed, however, that they would never solve their disagreements by fighting the old way. There would sometimes be a release of tension after all the yelling and screaming, but the relief was short-lived. Soon the tension would begin to build again, leading to another explosion. Instead, by directing their anger, they were able to resolve issues more quickly than they had ever done before, and without hurt feelings on either side. When anger is handled productively, it paves the way for positive feelings about yourself and others and leads ultimately to greater intimacy.

Listening to someone directly express his or her anger can be as unsettling as directing it yourself. You feel a great temptation to talk the person out of the feeling, convince the person that he or she is mistaken, or even attack back. When this happens, escalation is inevitable.

When you hear anger you are likely to feel criticized, rejected, or abandoned—not unlike how you may have felt as a child. Old baggage and yesterday's anger make it even more difficult to hear anger. These unresolved feelings leave you tense and defensive, like a mousetrap ready to snap. Old feelings become activated when someone expresses anger toward you. That's why it is important for you to express those feelings in a safe environment.

You may also have difficulty hearing anger because, as a child, you may have thought that anger meant hate. It is not uncommon for abusers to have two modes: calm and rage, or love and hate. So you learn that when someone expresses anger he or she is also saying, "I don't love you." However, it is possible to love someone and express anger at the same time. In fact, the willingness to express such a difficult emotion can itself be a demonstration of love. Therefore you need to remind yourself that when others express their anger at you it doesn't necessarily mean they hate you, that you're a bad person, or that they are going to abandon you. It only means they are upset. You have stepped on their toes. Like you, when they are angry they simply need to be heard and responded to appropriately.

Anger in Context

Anger is but one feeling that you have the capacity to experience. When you deny anger—or any feeling—it can undermine relationships and cause depression, acting out, or an inability to concentrate. Feelings usually travel in groups, and if there is anger, fear, hurt, and sadness are usually not far behind.

Most men find it harder to get in touch with fear, hurt, and sadness than with anger. Society permits men to express their anger, especially if it is accompanied by aggressive action. It may be tempting for you to stay angry and not delve down deeper into other feelings. Anger can make you feel powerful and intimate (when expressed appropriately), but it can also create distance and be used to intimidate others. Further, it is easy to stay angry, vengeful, and bitter if the alternative is to experience your deepest inner pain. Thus anger can serve as a defense against your other feelings. Healing means coming face to face with the pain. So learn about your anger, get comfortable with expressing yourself, but don't stop at that point.

You can stuff feelings of sadness, hurt, guilt, shame, and fear, and you may find extreme ways of avoiding them—alcohol, drugs, violence, or other self-destructive behaviors. Ultimately, if you cut yourself off from your feelings, you begin to feel alienated not only from others but from yourself. Getting in touch with these more vulnerable feelings is very difficult because you probably have never learned how to be sensitive to them. As with anger, however, getting in touch with and expressing them can actually bring you closer to people. Ironically, this can feel very threatening if you have learned through experience that getting close means getting hurt and trusting means being rejected. Jerry found this to be true for him.

When I first started expressing my anger it felt great. I was able to recognize it quickly and get it off my chest. When I came home at night, I was always expressing my anger about this or that. I was feeling great about getting my feelings out. There was only one thing: Everyone was terrified of me. My own family was afraid to say anything to me for fear of my rage. I was loud and intimidating in the name of being open and expressive. I realized that a lot of my anger was being fed by this incredible hurt inside from the abuse. Anger was a good start, but I got stuck there. I needed to go one step further. Expressing my hurt to my wife was really uncomfortable at first. I realized that there was a certain safety in being angry. Telling her about my other feelings brought up a whole new issue. What if she rejects me? What will she do with these feelings?

Although expressing his anger was important, Jerry needed to recognize that beneath this feeling were the hurt, sadness, and fear that were hidden long ago.

For Leonard, expressing these feelings is simply incongruent with his idea of being a man: "I just don't believe in men crying. I know that's fucked up, but that's how I feel. My father was like that. My grandfather was like that. And for all I know, his father was like that. If that's your goal in the counseling, I don't think I can do it."

You may have learned simply to numb yourself to your feelings, as Jerry did: "I was afraid when my father was home. I was afraid when he was not at home. I lived in a state of constant fear. After a while I just stopped feeling. Let me correct that; I stuffed my feelings. Otherwise, I wouldn't have been able to survive. At least I was able to focus on school and football. Today I have an ulcer, a daily reminder of my son-of-a-bitch father, who made me keep my anger inside."

Getting in Touch with Your Feelings

The process of getting in touch with any feeling, whether it's sadness, hurt, or fear, is very much like the one you used to recognize your anger. The best place to start is with your physical and behavioral cues.

Sam had a great deal of trouble getting in touch with his feelings of sadness. I knew he must have felt sad when his wife moved out, but he was unable to access the emotion. I suggested that he sit comfortably in his chair, take a few deep breaths, and close his eyes. Then I asked him to think about a time he had felt sad. What was the situation? Where did he feel the feelings in his body? How did he behave? I asked him to bring that feeling into his body right now. After a minute of silence, I asked him to open his eyes and tell me about his feelings:

I remember the time my wife left me because I wouldn't go to therapy. I came home and the house was completely empty. I felt this heaviness in my stomach. I wanted to cry, but I was afraid of what others would think of me. The crazy thing about it was that I was all alone. I couldn't even cry to myself. I felt so sad. It still makes me feel sad when I think about it.

That's how Sam began expressing his sadness: no fireworks, no drama, just sadness. The first time you deliberately get in touch with your feelings you probably won't experience a dramatic breakthrough. You may feel somewhat relieved afterward or it may be slow, subtle, and not immediately rewarding. Feelings sometimes need to be expressed piecemeal over an extended period of time before you begin to notice a difference.

If you are having trouble identifying times when you were feeling sad, hurt, or fearful, your partner or a friend may be able to help you pinpoint specific incidents. "Remember when you felt sad about your guitar being stolen? How about the time you felt afraid that your wife was going to leave you? I remember you felt hurt when I forgot your birthday." Frequently others recognize that we are feeling something before we do. We may be asked, "Are you okay?" or "Is there something wrong?" or "Did I hurt your feelings?" or "You seem sad [or hurt or frightened] right now." So, in addition to bodily cues, other people can sometimes indicate by their reactions you are feeling sad, frightened, or hurt.

You may get defensive when someone suggests you may be feeling something that you are either unaware of or don't want to communicate, especially when that other person is your partner. It may even feel like an invasion of privacy; "What is she trying to do, read my mind?" Although it may feel uncomfortable, try not to get defensive. If you are feeling something that you are not ready to talk about, just tell her, "Yes, I am upset about something, but I need some time to think about it before I talk with you. I will come to you when I am ready." Frequently your partner will recognize your feelings before you do. It's important to pay attention rather than get defensive. Maybe she senses something within you that you are unaware of. You could learn something about yourself by listening. It takes some self-confidence to let your partner help you in this way. It is an acknowledgment that she has something to offer you, and at the same time it doesn't mean that you are weak or less than her.

Communicating your feelings directly to others is an important aspect of healing. The formula is similar to that for directing anger.

Communicating Feelings

"I am feeling (sad, hurt, frightened, etc.) because _____ . I would like _____ ."

It is important to express your feelings specifically, when the situation calls for that response, so other people have no doubt about what is going on with you. This way the other person does not have to read your mind. You have probably felt frustrated when someone has expected you to know what they were thinking or feeling without telling you.

Asking for what you want is equally important because it lets other people know how to respond. Should they give advice, help you in some way, give you a hug, or simply listen? Here are a few examples how this formula may work in healing from childhood abuse.

- I am feeling sad because I've been having flashbacks about my father lately. I would like you just to know this so you are aware of why I may be acting a little low lately.

- I am feeling very scared telling you about the sexual abuse. I want you just to listen.

- I felt very hurt the other day when you told me to forget about the abuse. I want you to take me seriously by just listening without giving advice.

Words, however, are not the only means of communicating feelings. Each man has his own particular way of expressing feelings, which may be different from how women or other men express themselves. Some men can express themselves through actions, such as crying, becoming very quiet, drawing, writing, or being physically active. What's important is that you get your feeling out in the way most comfortable to you. Equally important is that your method is clear, direct, and doesn't infringe on the rights of others.

Learning to identify and communicate your feelings takes much practice. Paying attention to how other people communicate their feelings can help you learn new ways to express yourself. Each day it will become easier to recognize that when you are feeling that tension in your stomach you are frightened, or when you feel the sinking feeling in your chest you are sad, or when your breathing becomes lighter you're feeling depressed. Over time your awareness of your feelings will become greater. Taking the next step—expressing your feelings—is just as important to your healing. This is particularly helpful when discussing your childhood abuse with others. Even when you are alone you should learn to take your emotional temperature. How are you feeling about the abuse? About the person who perpetrated it? About others who may or may not have known about it?

Sometimes you may not want to communicate your feelings. It is important that you give yourself the time to sit with your feelings and get to know them. You can communicate them when you are ready. For some men, the process of identifying their feelings can take hours or days, and all the asking in the world by others is not going to speed that process. However, taking control of how and when you express yourself is particularly important. In the past that control was violated by your abuser. Today, however, you do have choices as to when and how you will communicate your feelings. In that way you can begin to feel less like a victim and more in charge of your life.

Don't forget: You will never stop having feelings. In fact, you will probably continue to have feelings about the abuse throughout your life. Over time, however, their intensity will somewhat diminish. Subsequently they will have less effect on your behaviors and attitudes. As you air out those old-baggage feelings from the abuse—whether they are anger, sadness, or hurt—they will cease to influence feelings that you experience today.

The feelings journal is one tool that can help you become better aware of your feelings. Writing down your feelings, even if they weren't verbally communicated, is healthy because you are not stuffing (denying) or escalating (blaming); you are stating them as fact—"I felt this way"—and you are getting them off your chest. The sooner you can write in your journal after the feeling, the better. Write in it every day. You can't go through a day without some feeling. Remember, you don't have to show anyone your journal. It's just for you.

The Feelings Journal

Your feelings may be minor: "I was irritated when I got caught in traffic." Or they may be more significant: "Today I felt hurt when my partner snapped at me." Feelings come in varying intensities. If you become overwhelmed by any emotion, use any one of the various techniques described in Chapter 2—meditation, drawing, and exercise can be effective ways to help yourself when you feel possessed by your emotions.

Learning to identify, communicate, and feel comfortable with emotions, like any skill, takes time and practice. So go easy on yourself. Be patient. Most important, give yourself credit for having the courage to confront a very difficult problem.

Chapter 6

HEALING THROUGH
YOUR ATTITUDES

An important part of the healing process involves coming to terms with how the abuse has affected your attitudes about yourself and others. As a child you probably received both subtle and not-so-subtle negative messages about your worth or value. This psychological abuse didn't necessarily stop when you left home. Wounded men often take with them these negative messages and as a result are carrying with them their own inner abuser. Negative messages are still running your life today.

Your inner abuser is the voice within you that calls you stupid or incompetent. He or she will criticize you at every opportunity. Your inner abuser will undermine your best efforts and attack you at every opportunity. It is important to become aware of how your inner abuser is activated—usually when you make the slightest mistake or make a minor error in judgment. When you try to accomplish a difficult task, he may be right there predicting how you are going to screw up or fail altogether. He may be most evident in your relationships. He may make you all too willing either to take all the blame for the problems in the relationship or to blame the other person for all the problems. Your inner abuser thrives on your serious problems, such as addiction and violence, because it gives him the opportunity to get on your case on a regular basis. Here are some common negative messages spoken by the inner abuser:

The Inner Abuser

- You can't do anything right.

- You're stupid.

- Your ugly.

- You're too fat [too skinny].

- You're not strong enough.

- You don't act like a man.

- You're unsuccessful.

- You don't make enough money.

- You are unlikeable.

- You are weak.

- You act like a sissy.

- You screwed up your marriage.

- Your kids hate you.

- You can't trust others.

- You can't trust yourself.

These negative messages, repeated over and over, inevitably result in low self-esteem. This will only reinforce your anger and distrust toward yourself and others, which may ultimately lead to feelings of depression, alienation, and isolation. You may not be consciously aware of your inner messages, but you may feel low self-esteem or distrust of others just the same. These feelings often lead to serious problems, such as violence, a critical attitude toward others, fear of communicating feelings, fear of asking for help when needed, social withdrawal, or dependence on chemicals. For healing to progress, these problems need to be addressed directly.

What Is Self-esteem?

Your self-esteem is made up of personal beliefs and messages that reflect how you value yourself. Self-esteem is either low or high, depending on the types of beliefs and messages. As a child, your sense of self-worth came from the adults in your life, primarily those in your family. You have probably incorporated subtle or overt negative messages accompanying your abusive experiences into your belief system. Self-esteem is an important issue for almost all men who were abused as children. Your attempts to stop or control the abuse most likely met with little success, which resulted in feelings of shame, impotence, helplessness, and incompetence.

Tom believed that he was a failure in life. He was a carpenter, not a physician like his father. He would frequently refer to himself as a loser. To make things worse, he felt responsible for all the problems in his marriage. He believed that he was worthless because of his problems, and as a result he constantly felt angry at himself and others. Evan was sexually abused by his mother. He believed that he was responsible for the abuse because to some extent he enjoyed the sensations. He repeated the cycle by fondling his niece on one occasion. Today he is depressed and feels that his life is not worth living, that he won't ever change. Andrew was neglected by his parents. In response, he developed a tough exterior. He learned how to use wit and intelligence to intimidate others and to reinforce a superior attitude. After a painful divorce, however, he discovered that his tough exterior was his attempt to compensate for his own lack of confidence and low self-esteem.

Blaming yourself yourself for the abuse is another manifestation of low self-esteem. We come to do this because we are either overtly blamed by our abuser or because others may criticize us for being "sexually provocative" or "a bad boy". However, children often blame themselves for their parents' unhappiness because they don't know better.

You may also have experienced psychological abuse in the form of name-calling, put-downs, and insults. You may have been conditioned to feel that you are only good for sex.

Self-esteem is an important issue for all men because we are constantly faced with male role models in television and film who portray the male ideal. Few of us can live up to that image and as a result we may feel somewhat inadequate.

Having internalized these messages you may discover that you play them back in your head over and over and over again. The result of this endless playback can be feelings of depression and anger, or destructive behaviors that serve only to lower self-esteem further.

Barry became depressed when things went wrong in his life. In order to lift himself out of his funk, he would drink. He would then escalate an argument to the point of violence, which would add to his belief that he was a failure. Dealing with his feelings would not be enough. He also needs to address his negative self-esteem, which only serves to intensify his feelings and ultimately cause behavior problems.

Why change low self-esteem? Because low self-esteem is self-abuse. Continuing to victimize yourself only perpetuates the cycle of violence. It manifests in destructive behaviors that only reinforce your negative attitudes. Eventually it will also affect others. Low self-esteem will cause you to gravitate toward others who also have a negative self-image. When two people in an intimate relationship have low self-esteem, there is a greater possibility that negative patterns of relating will emerge. If you ultimately want to heal your wounds, it is crucial to come to terms with your inner abuser.

Putting Yourself Down: Negative Self-talk

Negative self-talk messages are messages that put you down, minimize your positive qualities, or contribute to general feelings of depression, anger, or frustration. Negative self-talk are messages that play down your value as a human being. For example, "I'm a failure. I can't do anything right."

These messages come from our past, but we speak them in our own voice. Tony feels that his body is never good enough:

> I'm balding. I've been losing hair since I was nineteen. I'm overweight. I feel like a fat slob. I've always hated the way my face looked. My nose is too big. My ears stick out. I feel unattractive. I know where this came from. My father used to criticize my looks all the time. He would make me stand in front of the mirror naked and then would tear me apart verbally. I've been doing it ever since.

Negative self-talk can also be messages of self-blame or feeling responsible for other people's problems or even the abuse itself. Mark's parents were very unhappy. They would fight almost every night. Frequently they would fight about the kids. Mark felt responsible for their unhappiness, and he also felt responsible for their abuse of him:

> Back then, I thought if I would only do the right thing they would stop fighting and would be happy. I tried to get good grades, follow the rules at home, you know, just be good. But they would fight anyway. I did screw up at times and I would get the shit beaten out of me, usually with a belt, a hanger, or whatever was handy at the time. They would lay a guilt trip on me, telling me I was making their lives miserable. I believed it and

thought I deserved the abuse. It never crossed my mind that their misery had nothing to do with me. But I kept trying to make them happy. I was doing for them what they were supposed to be doing for me. Well, this pattern did not end when I left home. In fact, it got worse. I was always doing things to make other people happy, believing that my needs were not important. This pattern led to the downfall of most of my relationships. I never felt like I deserved to be happy. These tapes would play in my head: "My needs are not important." "Make everyone else happy." "Don't rock the boat." Then when things go wrong I take it all on myself. I punished myself for years afterwards. Until recently, it never dawned on me that I was just replaying my family dynamics.

List some of your own negative self-talk messages. Be specific. Are there messages specific to your work? What about your intimate relationships? Do you run these messages with friends or family? Do you blame yourself for being abused?

What Are Your Negative Self-talk Messages?

Many of these negative self-talk messages were recorded many years ago. They represent a part of the abuser that has been incorporated into your own psyche. These tapes don't belong to you, but you have kept them just the same, listening to them faithfully every day. Unfortunately, these tapes are trying to bring you down. you may even experience a downward spiral when you begin to start the tapes in your head. This is the mark of the inner abuser at work.

Getting to Know Your Inner Abuser

The inner abuser is most powerful when you do not recognize his presence. Therefore it is important that you come face to face with him. Doing so will make you more aware of how he affects you from day to day. The more conscious of him you become the better you will get at stopping a downward spiral of self-esteem. Over time he will have less and less influence over you.

The best way to get to know your inner abuser is by giving him a face and a name. In one of our sessions, I asked Barry to place his inner abuser on a chair in the middle of the room and describe him to me. He said that he looked something like an ape, with black hair all over and human facial qualities. His father had black hair and would tower over him and scream and yell like an ape before he would beat him severely. Jerry's inner abuser was clearly his father, a tall, muscular man in a three-piece suit. Evan was sexually abused by his mother. His inner abuser was a witch with long blond hair. Her name was Bitch.

Who Is Your Inner Abuser?

Visual imagery can be a useful tool in the healing process. This is not an exotic technique—you probably did it quite often as a child at play. So you already know how to do it, you just need to remember. Let your imagination run wild.

First, describe your image of your inner abuser. What does he or she look like? Be as specific as possible, down to the color of the hair and eyes, what he or she is wearing, and how he or she is sitting or standing. What name do you give this inner abuser? You may choose a name that describes the image, or it may be your name or the name of your actual abuser. Sketching or painting your image of your inner abuser will help you better visualize him or her.

The next step in getting to know your abuser is to enter into a dialogue with him. They may sound strange, but it will help you learn how to stop the negative self-talk messages when they begin. This is the first step in raising self-esteem. Barry's dialogue with his inner abuser, the ape, is a good first example:

BARRY: Well, I've been listening to you a lot these days. You put me down. Treat me like shit. Who do you think you are? [Barry has made the decision to take charge of his inner abuser.] I've been listening to you for thirty years and I'm tired of it. I'm not going to let you ruin my life anymore.

APE: Barry, I'm your old friend. You need me to keep you from getting too happy and confident. You know that you tend to get out of control with that temper of yours. And you are not doing that well at work or at home. Come on, Barry, you need me to keep you in line.

BARRY: I don't need you to keep me in line. In fact, you're the one that gets me out of line. It's your negative messages that keep me down. I'm tired of being abused. I don't need it anymore.

APE: What would you do without me?

BARRY: I don't need you. I'm tired of being abused by you.

APE: Let's make a deal. [The ape is beginning to back down.]

BARRY: I don't want to make a deal. I'm in charge, not you!

Barry then described to me how it felt to talk with his inner abuser:

At first it felt awkward. I mean, it was like talking to myself. But then I realized how powerful these messages really are. He does exist inside of me. Talking with him has helped me really see who he is and how he tries to affect me. I've got to take control or he will, and I certainly don't want to see what that would be like.

Consider asking your inner abuser these questions to begin with:

- Who are you?

- Where did you come from?

- What messages do you give me?

- What do you get out of your negative messages?

Then you may want to tell your inner abuser how you are feeling about him. You may want to challenge your inner abuser point by point on each message. This is your opportunity to take charge and not be pushed around anymore.

Positive Self-Talk

You can overcome the work of your inner abuser through positive self-talk. Positive self-talk raises self-esteem, deescalates anger and depression, and brings about more uplifting feelings. It sets limits on how much your inner abuser is going to influence you.

Positive self-talk is neither inflated nor deflated; it is a realistic assessment of yourself. Everyone has both positive and negative qualities. Positive self-talk doesn't focus on one or the other.

The word *affirmation* is often used to describe positive self-talk. An affirmation is a statement or assertion about yourself that is hopeful, optimistic, and empowering.

For example, a negative self-talk message such as "Boy I screwed up this time. I'm really stupid" can be made into positive self-talk or an affirmation: "I made a mistake and I am going to learn from it." The positive self-talk statement includes the fact that you made a mistake; this is a realistic assessment of the situation. But it also includes a positive interpretation of the event: We can all learn from our mistakes. Let's take several more examples:

NEGATIVE: "I'm fucked up for beating up my wife."
POSITIVE: "I have a serious problem with my temper. I have become violent with my wife. I need to learn how to control my anger."

NEGATIVE: I'm just a drunken asshole."
POSITIVE: "I have an alcohol problem. I need help before I hurt myself or others."

NEGATIVE: "The abuse screwed me up. No one will want to be with me."
POSITIVE: "The abuse has affected me in some ways, but I also have positive qualities. People will see those qualities in me. Everyone has problems. At least I am working on solving mine."

Can You Transform Negative Self-talk to Positive Self-talk?   Look over the negative messages you came up with in the earlier exercise. Transform those statements into positive self-talk messages. Remember, positive self-talk includes a realistic assessment of the circumstance as well as a positive interpretation of the situation.

The most common type of negative self-talk for victims of child-hood abuse is self-blame for the abuse.

Liberating
Yourself from
the Abuse

You may be blaming yourself directly by telling yourself or others, "I caused the abuse." Or it may be more subtle, such as "I was a seductive child" or "I was always causing trouble." Look back at the rationalizations in Chapter 4. Some of these may be internal statements that you run in your mind to blame yourself for the abuse. Self-blame perpetuates feelings of depression, anger, shame, and low self-esteem. If you believe that you were somehow to blame for the abuse, healing will be very difficult. In order to break your low self-esteem pattern you must let yourself off the hook. You can do this by telling yourself that you were not to blame for the abuse. You were a child at the time. There is no justification for an adult to hurt a child. This is why, today, child abuse is against the law.

Telling yourself that you were not responsible for the abuse doesn't mean that you are not responsible for changing how the abuse affected you. As an adult, you need to take responsibility for your problems by seeking help and changing destructive patterns of behavior.

Saying to yourself or out loud that you were not responsible for the abuse is a powerful positive self-talk message. Say it out loud. How does it feel to say the words? Do you believe them? Repeat the statement several times. Even if you don't believe it you can begin by acting as though you do. How would you behave differently if you *really* believed that you were not responsible for the abuse?

Can You Tell Yourself, "I Was Not Responsible for the Abuse?"

Improving self-esteem is like having a garden. If you don't pay attention to it, weeds grow, plants die, and before you know it, your garden is a mess. In order to prevent this from happening, you need to go out there every day and pick out the weeds, use fertilizer, and take care of the plants.

Other Ways to Improve Self-esteem

Improving your self-esteem takes the same kind of effort. You need to do things that make you feel good about yourself. How about the fence you have wanted to put up in the backyard? What about the furniture that's been needing repair? How long has it been since you've been out for a run or played tennis? Does waxing and cleaning the car make you feel good? What about a hike at your favorite beach or state park? When was the last time you lay in your hammock and just relaxed? For some men, having alone time can be energizing. Have you been wanting to volunteer at a community organization? Have you been spending quality time with your family lately? When was the last time you expressed appreciation to your child, partner, or a friend? How about a date with a close friend? Going into therapy can also be a constructive way to improve self-esteem.

Doing things for yourself and others can make you feel good about yourself. That's what it's all about. What can you do today to raise your self-esteem?

Trusting Yourself and Others

One characteristic that seems to find itself on wounded men's negative lists relates to the issue of trust—trusting oneself and trusting others. If you can't trust yourself, you'll have a great deal of difficulty trusting others. Without trust, your ability to have close, successful, intimate relationships will be greatly limited. This will only give your inner abuser ammunition to make you feel worse about yourself. How do you begin to address this issue? By listening to your inner abuser.

Is there a voice within you that says, Don't trust anyone? If there is, it is because as a child you trusted a person and that trust was betrayed. You didn't have the rational ability to say to yourself, I can't trust this person. Instead, you may generalize your experience to say, I can't trust men, I can't trust women, or I can't trust anyone. The world is not a safe place. In the early stages of development, children learn about the concept of trust and form what will be lifelong attitudes about it. An experience with abuse can skew a young person's image of trust, particularly of persons with whom they are supposed to feel safe. These attitudes about trust are taken into every relationship and can profoundly effect your interactions with others. You need to learn how to challenge this suspicious voice in order to discover how to trust others.

Do you trust yourself? If not you may also have begun to question whether or not you are capable of making good choices about whom you can and can't trust.

Trust is the cornerstone of any close or intimate relationship. Without it there can be no real communication, no safety in being yourself. Lack of trust accounts for most of the problems that couples experience and, more important, it is the reason why so many couples are unable to solve their disagreements and subsequently break up. Likewise, if you don't trust your inner radar, that is, your thoughts, feelings, and needs, you are likely to get yourself into situations that are unhealthy or even down right dangerous.

Learning to Trust Yourself

Learning to trust begins with trusting yourself. What you learned in the previous chapter about feelings and needs is an important part of this task. Trusting yourself involves believing in your heart that your feelings (anger, hurt, sadness, etc.) and inner needs (for affection, understanding, help, etc.) are valid and need to be expressed and responded to. Likewise, learning how to trust your perceptions of others is equally important, especially when it comes to intimate relationships. If you sense something is a problem but don't validate your perception and address it, you could find yourself in over your head before realizing what you got yourself into.

Mark was sexually abused by his uncle, with whom he spent a great deal of time. They would talk, go for hikes, and fish together. His uncle bought them season tickets to the Dodgers games. For many years he believed he had found a great adult friend in his uncle. Mark trusted him with his thoughts and feelings. His uncle first began to convince Mark to take showers with him. These led to massages and rub-downs. These led to fondling and eventually anal intercourse. The progression occurred over a number of years. Mark began to avoid his uncle and eventually stopped seeing him altogether. But this was not until Mark mustered up the courage to break off their relationship. His uncle betrayed Mark's trust in him. Twenty years later, when Mark entered counseling to deal with a failed marriage and alcoholism, he disclosed the experiences. Mark came to realize that his experience not only greatly affected his trust of his wife and others but, most important, he lacked trust in himself. He explained:

> I was so blown away by that experience I really began to question my ability to choose trustworthy people as friends. How could I have been so blind to this guy? I realize intellectually that there was no way of knowing, but in my heart I keep asking myself, Why didn't you see it coming? When he began to touch me in ways that felt uncomfortable I would pull away, and he would try to convince me it was okay that we were doing this. I listened to him because he was a grownup. He was my friend. He wouldn't have hurt me. If I had listened to my gut I would have run away and never returned. To this day I still don't listen to my gut. I can't trust my own judgment about others. When I meet someone, I don't pay attention to what I'm feeling inside so I passively submit to whatever they want. As a result, I've gotten into some really screwed-up relationships in my life. I want to learn how to trust myself, but I don't know where to begin.

Like Mark, your lack of inner trust may be evident in your inability to choose healthy relationships.

Lack of self-trust could also result in never having your needs met. For example, Steven had great difficulty asking others for help. On one hand, he rationally knew that it was normal to need assistance at various times. On the other hand, he had an irrational fear of others judging him for not knowing how to do something or needing their help. He wanted others to think he was competent and independent. In spite of his needs, he would continue on his own, sometimes creating more problems than he had initially. This was especially evident when he attempted to fix his car on his own.

The more he tried to do it himself, the more it ultimately cost him when he got in over his head.

Lack of self-trust could also result in your not being able to set limits with others. Larry had a great deal of difficulty with this issue. He would say yes when he really meant no. Whenever anyone asked for volunteers or a favor, he was the first in line. He would agree to do something even when he knew deep down inside that he was already overloaded or simply uninterested. As a result, he was always taking on more than he could handle. He would frequently get physically sick from being burned out. At other times he would rebel and become completely irresponsible, letting people down who were counting on him.

Trusting your perceptions of others and of your own needs and limits is critical to having high self-esteem and, ultimately, healthy relationships. Otherwise you are constantly taking care of others at the expense of your own needs. Additionally, it is important to verbalize your needs so others do not have to read your mind. It is important to learn how to trust your gut-feeling response and to honor it. This means learning to saying no when your gut tells you no and learning how to speak up when the little voice inside you says, Hey, you, wake up, I need something.

Trusting Others

How does this lack of trusting yourself manifest in an intimate relationship? Many wounded men are fearful of expressing their inner needs and feelings. As a result there is lack of communication. This includes not discussing highly charged topics such as child-hood abuse. Are you fearful of talking about the abuse with your partner? Do you fear your partner's judgment of you or, worse, complete rejection? Are you afraid of appearing weak or crazy? Do you think your relationship can endure a disclosure such as this? Perhaps you fear that your partner doesn't have the time for your problems.

Bret was sexually abused by his father. He came into therapy because of sexual problems in his marriage. After disclosing the abuse to me it took him several months before he built up the courage to tell his wife. When I asked him why he was afraid he told me:

> She'll think I'm nuts. Sometimes I think I'm nuts. I don't know what she'll think of me. Maybe she'll think I'm making a big deal out of nothing or that I'm really homosexual. I don't even feel comfortable with this, how can she? What if she leaves me?

Don't underestimate the strength of your relationship. If there is a foundation of caring, love, and mutual respect the relationship can handle this problem. It may make things rocky for a while. There may even be times when you regret having said anything at all. But in the end, it can strengthen the bond beyond your wildest fantasies. If your partner is interested in you, then she is going to be interested in your problems and your feelings. Don't use your fears as an excuse for not taking a step to develop trust in your relationship.

Learning to Trust

Learning how to trust yourself and others is like any other skill—it takes both practice and the belief that change is possible. Learning to trust begins with listening to and honoring your inner positive voices and challenging the negative ones. It also involves taking risks by communicating both verbally and nonverbally your needs and feelings. It requires both an objective and a subjective point of view. The subjective involves getting in touch with your inner self and ultimately making contact with another person. This gives you valuable information about how much you are trusting yourself. The objective part involves watching how others respond to your risk taking, which gives you valuable information about how much you can trust others. The more you trust yourself, the more you'll learn how to trust others. The more you learn how to trust, the better you'll feel about yourself and others.

Listening to the Voice Within

How do you learn to trust? The first step is to listen to the inner voices within you. One voice is telling you how you are feeling and the needs you have. Another voice may be telling you that your feelings and needs are stupid or unimportant. Or that others will judge you harshly—that they can't be trusted. Is this the work of your inner abuser?

Tony was physically abused by both his mother and stepfather. When he began to listen to his inner voices he reported the following:

I sat quietly after returning home from our last session and I began to listen. Sure enough, I could hear the voices loud and clear. One said, I am feeling alone with this information (about the abuse) and I need to tell Evelyn. The other said Don't trust anyone, Tony. Especially Evelyn. The world is a dangerous place. Remember what it was like growing up in your family? If you let her in, she'll hurt you. Stay strong, Tony, don't be a sissy. Besides, it's not safe.

Challenging the Inner Voice

That inner negative voice of yours is similar to the negative self-talk messages and the inner abuser. You need to confront the voice or it will negatively effect your relationships with others. So the next step in the process is challenging the belief system. One way of challenging that inner voice is through affirmations and positive self-talk. Positive statements such as "I can learn to trust this person" can counteract these negative messages by increasing your confidence and hopefulness. Likewise you need to remind yourself that your feelings and needs, no matter how big or little, are valid and important. A change in attitude can be encouraged by a change in behavior. This means taking risks, little risks at first.

Taking Risks

Taking risks involves behaviors that demonstrate that you are acting "as if" you trust. What does acting "as if" involve? Communication is one of the best indicators of trust between two people—not the communication per se but the manner and content of the communication.

Risk taking involves communicating thoughts and feelings that are otherwise difficult to share with others. When you do this you make yourself vulnerable. If you watch the other person's reaction when you make yourself vulnerable, you will receive important information about whether or not you can trust that particular person. So, by not playing it "safe," you can learn whom you can and whom you cannot trust. As with any communication, the chances of your needs being met are increased if you are able to say ahead of time what you want from that person. For example, "I just need you to listen" or "I need to be held" or "I need your help solving this problem."

Nonverbal communication is another way you may act "as if" you trust your partner. This type of communication can be in the form of touching. This is especially true if you find physical touch very anxiety provoking. Mark was physically and sexually abused. For him, touch of any kind, sexual or nonsexual, carries with it many negative associations. When he and his wife entered couples counseling they both identified this as a problem but from slightly different perspectives. Mark stated that Ellen was always coming on to him sexually. His wife, Ellen, stated that she understands about his fear of sex but she just wants "plain nonsexual physical affection." Mark never wants to touch at all." She tries to put her arm around him and he always pulls away. Mark was very open about his lack of trust in this area but as he stated, "Understanding this doesn't change how I feel."

I explained to both how trust begins with small steps rather than giant leaps. I also talked with Mark about his inner voice and how he needed to act "as if," if he wanted to learn to trust. I asked them if they were willing to try an experiment. I had them sit facing each other. I asked Ellen to put her hands on her lap. I told Mark, "When you feel comfortable I would like you to put your hands on top of hers." Within a few seconds he put his hands on top of hers. I asked him, "When you feel comfortable, would you hold her hands?" He then held her hands. I asked them to tell each other how they felt holding hands. Ellen said she felt good. Mark agreed. I told them both to just sit there and enjoy the contact. Then I had them reverse roles. Mark had his hands on his lap and Ellen put hers on top of his and then held them. Ellen expressed fear in making Mark feel uncomfortable. Mark said it did feel uncomfortable but he wanted to overcome the feeling. He told her to keep holding on.

From that session on, things progressed from hand holding to walking arm in arm to arms around shoulders and hugging. Ellen and Mark learned that going slowly would meet his need comfort while at the same time Ellen could get the affection she needed. They also learned that they had to communicate more with each other both verbally and physically. Mark needed to take risks in order to overcome his lack of trust, and he would would have to open up about the abuse and his feelings that were still ever present. He also needed to challenge his inner voice and take a chance with Ellen. In doing so, he was able to break through his barriers to trust. And you can do the same.

What types of risks can you take in your relationship to build trust? What thoughts, feelings, or needs can you communicate with your partner? In what nonverbal ways can you take a risk in your relationship?

Can You Take Risks?

For example:

I need to tell my partner about the abuse I experienced as a child. I have a lot of anger and hurt inside that would be hard to express. I'm not so worried about her reaction as I am worried about how I'd feel afterwards. Well, I guess if I was honest, I'd say I was a little afraid of her reaction. I just want her to listen to me. Maybe if we set up a time after the kids are asleep to talk for a while I could talk with her about it.

I hate getting massages. It reminds me of when my father abused me. I rationally know that Barbara is not going to hurt me but my body gets real tense. If I took a risk, I'd let her give me a short and light massage. Maybe if I told her specifically how to do it I would feel a little more comfortable.

Rebuilding Trust

Trust is easy to lose and difficult to rebuild. This is especially so when you or your partner has actually done things to engender a lack of trust. Have you done things that have contributed to a lack of trust in your relationship? For example, have you been judgmental, unsupportive, abusive, untruthful, or unreliable? If this is the case for you or your partner, both people need to make a concerted effort to pay attention to trust-building behavior. This is particularly so when abuse has been perpetrated or a marital agreement has been violated. Rebuilding trust takes time. Following through on agreements, staying open, expressing feelings, being consistent, providing information, working on your problems, admitting your difficulties, and keeping the lines of communication open will all serve to help rebuild trust. Each of these could be considered a heroic deed and therefore could also help to build self-esteem. Most important, you need to keep talking about the trust issue. Both partners need to discuss frequently how they are feeling toward each other in the trust department. Beyond this, time will eventually heal the wound so that it doesn't continually interfere with intimacy and love.

Chapter 7

HEALING THROUGH BEHAVIORS

Wounded men are likely to have behavior problems that range from violence and addictions to marital/relationship conflict, sexual difficulties, commitment problems, and general communication troubles. In fact, it is often a behavioral problem, such as spousal abuse, that drives men to seek out help.

Often the most difficult work of healing comes in trying to change these patterns of behavior. First, they are well embedded, and second, feelings, attitudes, and behaviors and inextricably linked. During the healing process you will discover the inner attitudes and feelings that motivate your particular behavioral problem. If you work on all three levels—feelings, attitudes, and behaviors—you will begin to notice changes.

Change doesn't come quickly for most men. But if you take small steps every day, setting out reasonable, attainable goals, your behaviors will change over time. Perfection won't come overnight, but progress on a daily basis is definitely possible. Once again, don't be afraid to ask for help.

Abuse and Power

The issues of power and powerlessness can help you understand why you may have learned to hurt yourself or others. As an abused child you experienced a tremendous feeling of powerlessness. You felt—and rightly so because of your size—that you were unable to stop the perpetrator. Having once felt powerless, the desire to feel powerful can seem to have a tremendous appeal. As an adult you may have been drawn to a similar situation in order to reenact your own victimization—but this time you are the one who has the power. Sam describes how his abuse of his wife was a way of feeling powerful in the face of powerlessness:

> The last time I battered my wife she was yelling at me about not fixing her car like I had been promising her for six weeks. I felt like she was telling me how bad I was and that I was going to get punished. It reminded me of my father, who was always beating me physically and mentally. All I could think was, I am not going to take this any longer. Now I can do something about it. I was going to stop her. So I did!

If you feel particularly powerless with other adults you may ultimately to turn to children, where feeling powerful is much easier. Bret, who was in treatment for sexually abusing his ten-year-old stepdaughter, tells how his own victimization may have partly accounted for his becoming a victimizer:

> I was sexually abused by my father from the age of eight or nine years old until he divorced my mother when I was thirteen. He may have done it before but I just don't remember, or I don't want to remember. He used to come into my room after

everyone was asleep and would get me hard and suck on me. It felt good in some ways but at the same time I felt really dirty and sick. He used to tell me not to tell anyone because they would think I was a queer. So I never said anything. In fact, I never talked about it until I was arrested. I remember there were times when I was fondling my daughter that I would actually be thinking about my father telling me that I was queer. I never really connected the two. I think I was trying to do two things when I was abusing my daughter. First, I did it to a girl to prove to myself that I wasn't queer, even though I had thoughts about doing it to a boy in the past. But second, and I think most important, I did it to her because I could control her. I couldn't control my father, I couldn't even control my wife. She was the only one I could control. But she was smart. She blew the whistle on me. Maybe if I taught her one thing right, it was to recognize bullshit when she saw it.

It is important to feel powerful, but it's crucial to understand the difference between feeling powerful and having power over others. Feeling powerful means feeling self-assured, aware of your feelings and beliefs, and being able to communicate them with others. You are empowered by self-confidence and knowledge that you can successfully assert your feelings and needs.

Power also comes in gaining mastery over your own self-destructiveness or unhealthy patterns. Your attempt to control others is no different than your abuser's control over you. Learning to control your abusive tendencies is an important step toward self-empowerment.

Violence Toward Others

You may be asking yourself, How could I hurt others as I was hurt? The answer is that violence begets violence.

As an abused child you probably stuffed your feelings for many years. You may have low self-esteem and a general distrust of those close to you. You almost certainly didn't learn healthy ways of dealing with the anger, hurt, frustration, and conflict that are bound to arise in any intimate relationship. In fact, having witnessed or been a victim directly of violence, you may have learned firsthand that violence is a viable solution to problems. Add to these patterns a chemical addiction and you have all the elements necessary for continuing the cycle of violence.

Now the power to stop the generational cycle of abuse is in your hands. By applying the skills you are learning in this book to everyday living situations you can break this cycle of abuse. You know intimately the devastation that occurs when you are abused by someone you trust. Getting in touch with these feelings can motivate you to put an end to the violence. In this way you are not only healing yourself but you are contributing to a much-needed change in society.

Experts in the field of chemical dependency say that each alcoholic affects at last four other people. Likewise, a wounded man who has perpetuated the cycle of violence is not only affecting himself but those around him. Each time you abuse another person you are giving yourself more ammunition for the inner abuser to say "You see, you really are a bad person." On a practical level you run the risk of being arrested and thrown in jail. But far worse is the fact that you negatively affect the lives of both the victims and the witnesses. If you abuse your spouse, she may turn around and abuse the kids out of sheer frustration. If you abuse your kids, they may grow up to become child or spouse abusers. The costs to both yourself and others are too high to continue to deny your problem.

Controlling Abusive Behaviors

Breaking Denial

The first step in learning to control your own abusive behaviors is to break denial by acknowledging to yourself and others that you are acting in an abusive manner. Admitting that your behavior is out of bounds is an important first step in self-control. You may have a great deal of trouble taking this first step, especially if you believe that it is a sign of weakness to admit hat you are having problems at home. It is much easier to blame your partner or the kids than to take personal responsibility. In fact, it may have taken a drastic situation, such as an arrest, for you to be willing to examine your problems.

Can you acknowledge to yourself that your behavior is out of control, that you have become violent with your spouse or a child? Can you acknowledge this to your partner and family? Give specific examples of the types of violence you have perpetrated and on whom.

Taking Responsibility

The next step to learning self-control is to realize that you are responsible for behaviors. You will have to change yourself, not others. Other people in your family may have problems, but you need to recognize that the only person who can control your behavior is you.

You may have tried to control your violence by trying to control the feelings, attitudes, or behaviors of others. We do this because we believe that if we can stop others from doing things that upset us we won't feel our own emotions. If this is true for you, you may have already realized that it has limited success. In truth we can control only our own behaviors. Even your emotional responses to situations are not in your control, though you can control how or if you show your feelings.

One of my clients complained, "You can't vote on your feelings!" If you feel angry, hurt, or sad you can't convince yourself that it is not so. You can take a walk, write about them, or talk about them, but you can't talk yourself out of them. Nor can you control the feelings of your partner or children. If they feel something, you can't talk them out of their feelings. You can be supportive and caring, which may help them get through the feelings sooner, but ultimately it's their decision what they are going to do with their feelings. The list of things you can't control is long: the future, the past, whether or not your relationship will work out, whether or not your partner will leave you (or return if she has already left). But you can control your behavior.

Recognizing that you are totally responsible for your behavior is probably the most difficult step you'll take in learning to control your violence. The temptation to blame your partner, children, boss, or police is so great that most men succumb to it. However, until you take complete responsibility for your behavior you will never be able to assure yourself or your family that the violence will stop. Only you can stop your abusive behaviors. Although the abuse occurs within a context, such as an argument with your spouse or child, it is still your choice to behave that way. Certainly there were times when you felt angry or hurt and you chose not to become violent. You make choices every day to behave in various ways. Sometimes you choose to ignore an issue or person; sometimes we choose to talk something out calmly; sometimes you choose to yell it out; and sometimes you choose to act it out. It's your choice.

I know it feels sometimes as if your violence is not a choice. Sometimes it feels as though your partner is pushing buttons, pulling strings, or turning a switch off and on. You may actually believe that you are being seduced or provoked into acting in an abusive manner. Yet you can deliberate and think about how you want to respond to your inner feelings. Your response will ultimately affect how you'll feel about yourself and how your partner and family will feel about you later.

Can you take responsibility for your violence? Try completing the following sentence: I recognize that I am responsible for my behavior when I _____ . For example:

- I recognize that I am responsible for my behavior when I slap my wife.

- I recognize that I am responsible for my behavior when I hit my child with a belt.

- I recognize that I am responsible for my behavior when I touch my niece in inappropriate ways.

If your goal is to stop being abusive toward others, then you need to learn how to solve interpersonal problems without violence. One common technique is called the time-out.

Taking a Time-out

The time-out works by separating you and the potential victim so that you can cool off, calm down, and rationally decide how you can deal with your feelings. When you begin to experience strong feelings of anger, frustration, anxiety (or any feeling for that matter), or if you find yourself acting abusive, say to your partner, "I'm beginning to feel angry and I'm going to take a time-out." Then leave the situation for an hour. Do something physical like taking a walk, run, or bicycle ride. The time-out is not a time to socialize but to be by yourself and calm yourself down. This may be an excellent time for you to write in your feelings log. It is also important not to use any mood-altering chemicals, such as alcohol or other drugs. You want to be more in control, not less. After the hour is up, return and talk about what you were feeling. If you begin to feel yourself getting out of control again, take another time-out. Use the time-out procedure as much as possible during the early stages of healing. This means that you may not completely solve all of your problems for a while, but at least you will stop one big one, your violence.

You can also use the time-out if you are abusing a child. If you are getting into a power struggle, then you may want the child to take a time-out by placing the child in his or her room to sit quietly for an hour to calm down. Afterward you and the child can discuss how to better solve the problem in the future. If you feel you are about to lose control, you may want to take a time-out (make sure you have an agreement with your partner to watch the child during your cooling-down period). No matter how you use the time-out, it is important for you to explain the procedure to your partner and children so that they know how and why it works.

The time-out helps you learn how to better manage your feelings. Don't forget, the level of feeling you experience may be greater than the current situation seems to justify because of old baggage that is mixed in with the present crisis. The intensity of your feelings may be too great for you to handle without a cooling-down period, but cooling down alone may not be enough to help you regain control. Anger can be stubborn and can take some time to simmer down. Learning to use your thinking function can help this process along.

As we have seen, rebuilding trust is an important first step in the violence-recovery process. Taking a time-out helps rebuild that trust. The key is threefold: Honesty, openness, and willingness. Honesty: You are saying that you are feeling angry. You are being honest with your feelings. You say that you are going to take a time-out and you do it. You say that you are going to be gone for an hour and you return in an hour. Consistency between words and actions helps to build trust. Openness: You are open to using a new technique. You are open to your partner's or child's need for safety. Willingness: You are willing to go to any lengths to stop your violence. This means putting aside your need to win an argument or make a point for the greater need of nonviolence in your family. The time-out not only rebuilds trust with others, it also teaches you how to trust yourself to control your destructive impulses.

Talking Yourself Down Controlling your feelings may take more than removing yourself from the situation. You may have to talk yourself down. One benefit of being human is having the ability to both feel and think. Depending on the situation, one may be more important than the other, but being able to use both functions is important.

Earlier we discussed stuffing, escalating, and directing. You have probably used these methods to cope with all your feelings, including anger. Talking yourself down is similar to directing. When you direct, the potential for violence immediately diminishes. Simply telling yourself that you are feeling angry, hurt, or sad will help you lower the intensity of your feelings, and you will be less likely to act out those feelings violently.

Talking yourself down also involves strategizing productive ways of dealing with feelings: staking a time-out, getting some physical exercise, meditating, doing relaxation exercises, writing in your feelings log, or simply going outside for fresh air. Directing and strategizing help you think of alternatives to violence, and the very process decreases the intensity of your feelings. The time-out is an opportunity for you to talk yourself down rather than stuff or escalate. When you return from the time-out, you are less upset than when you left. The time-out and talking yourself down are both anger-management techniques that can help you stop your violence. As a result you will feel better and others will feel better about you.

Communication skills can also help preventing violent acting-out. Communicating your feelings and needs—learning how to ask for what you want and how to say no—is very important. If you have directed your abuse toward your child, you may need to learn about healthy child development, parenting skills, maintaining intimacy in relationships, examining sex-role attitudes, and clarifying relationship expectations. Use the feelings log, meditation, creative outlets, and physical exercise (all described in Chapter 2) to deescalate your anger and avoid a violent outburst. The more skills you possess, the less likely you are to choose violence when confronted with a difficult situation.

The bottom line is that violence is a choice. You need to make a conscious decision to choose other alternatives. The healing process has many aspects, but the most important is immediately to address the destructive, violent behaviors so that you and others are safe. Once you bring your violence under control you can heal your feelings and attitudes in order to remain violence free.

Addictions: Chemical and Process

Wounded men are prone to addiction because of the need to suppress or avoid strong feelings. There is a high correlation between addiction and abuse and you may have learned addictive patterns of coping with problems by observing your parent or abuser. If you have an addictive pattern in your life, you are less likely to face your inner wounds. Therefore it is crucial to your healing journey that you take the first step in breaking the cycle of addiction.

How to Stop Violence - NOW!*

The Time-out is a guaranteed method for stopping the violence from now on. This method has been used successfully by many men and all it takes is your Time-out: Whenever you feel your anger rising, your body tensing as if it is going to explode, or that you are frustrated or out of control, say out loud to yourself and your wife or lover:

"I'm beginning to feel angry and I need to take a time-out."

Leave your home for one hour (no longer and no shorter), during which you cannot drink or use drugs and you should not drive (unless it is absolutely necessary). It is most preferable for you to go for a walk or run, to do something physical. If you begin to think about the situation that made you angry, just say to yourself, I'm beginning to feel angry and I need to take a time-out. In this way you will be taking a mental time-out as well as a physical time-out.

When you return in one hour, check in and tell your partner that you have come back from your time-out and ask if she would like to talk with you. If you *both* want to discuss the situation, tell her what it was that made you feel angry. You may also want to talk about what it was like for you to take a time-out. If one of you doesn't want to talk about the situation, respect that person's need not to discuss it. In either case, if you find yourself feeling angry again, take another time-out.

Some topics of conversation may be too charged to talk about. If this is true in your situation, put that issue on the shelf for a while, acknowledging that it is too difficult for the two of you to discuss alone. Take these issues and others to a counselor to get some help working them out. Even if it's an important issue that is making you angry, think of your priorities. Nothing can be more important than stopping the violence!

How Time-outs Work

Let's now look at the different aspects of the time-out to see how and why it works.

*This and other techniques are covered more thoroughly in my earlier book, *Learning to live without violence: A handbook for men*. (Volcano, Calif.: Volcano Press, 1989).

I'm . . .

An "I" statement. You begin by talking about yourself, and talking about yourself immediately puts you in charge of yourself. You aren't name-calling or blaming.

. . . Beginning to Feel Angry . . .

You are talking about how you feel. It's a direct communication. Nothing unclear about this statement. Saying you feel angry may in fact make you feel less angry. Try it—you'll like it!

. . . I need to Take a Time-out . . .

Another "I" statement. You are also saying to your partner that you are not going to hit her; instead, you're going to do something else, take a time-out. Taking a time-out helps build up trust with the other person by showing that in fact there will be no violence.

. . . Leave for an Hour . . .

If you stay away for the full hour, you and she should be sufficiently cooled off by the time you return.

. . . Don't Drink, Use Drugs, or Drive . . .

Drinking and drugs will only make the situation worse. Don't drive, because there are already enough angry people on the roads!

. . . Do Something Physical . . .

Going for a walk, a run, or a ride on your bicycle will help discharge some of the angry tension in your body.

. . . Come back in an Hour—no Sooner, no Later . . .

If you agree to come back in an hour, live up to your agreement. It helps to build trust. In addition, an hour will give you enough time to cool off.

. . . Check in—Talk about What It
Was That Made You Angry . . .

If you do no more than check in, you will have completed the exercise. If you go on to talk about what it was that made you angry, you get experience and practice in communicating and discussing emotional issues.

When there has been violence in a relationship, the trust factor drops significantly. This time-out exercise not only helps stop the violence but also helps rebuild trust. Trust takes some time to rebuild. Just because you may take one or two time-outs, it doesn't mean that everything is okay. Be patient! Concentrate on identifying your anger and taking your time-outs. The rest takes time.

IMPORTANT: Be sure to tell your wife or lover about the time-out and how it works. You might even want to read this chapter aloud and talk about it together. No matter which way you do it, be sure she understands what the time-out is and how and why it works.

Time-outs Are Hard to Do!

Why? Because men grow up to believe that only a coward will walk away from a fight. Your impulse will be to stay and finish it, or at least get in

Most people think about alcohol and other drugs when they hear the word "addiction." However, addiction is more general than just alcoholism or drug addiction. It refers to any habit or dependence on a chemical or process that can potentially create serious problems in your life. You can develop a psychological addiction to just about any substance and a physical addiction to many substances that we ordinarily think of as healthy or harmless.

You may, of course, be addicted to a mood-altering chemical. The most common are alcohol, marijuana, cocaine, opiates (such as heroin), amphetamines (speed), hallucinogens (such as acid), and barbiturates (downers). Prescription drugs—muscle relaxants (such the last word. But think of what is most important to you. Is it important to maintain your image as a "real man" or to stop the violence?

Many men have also expressed the fear that their partners will be gone when they return. This is part of the trust building; as each of you follows through with your part in the time-out, the trust will grow.

The only frequent problem men have with time-outs is staying away from alcohol. Many people use alcohol to treat loneliness, and you may feel quite alone during your time-out. Men will often go to a bar to hang out with their buddies when they need support or someone to talk to. We want to emphasize again that alcohol and drugs can make an argument much worse.

Although taking time-outs may be difficult for you initially, they will get easier if you take practice time-outs. Practice time-outs are the same as real time-outs except for two things: First, in a practice time-out you are *not* feeling angry. Second, the practice time-out is only half an hour. It's just practice at saying the words and walking away. You tell your partner, "I'm *NOT* beginning to feel angry but I want to take a practice time-out." The more you take practice time-outs, the easier it will be to take real time-outs.

as Valium), narcotics (such as Demerol), amphetamines (such as diet pills), barbiturates (such as sleeping pills), and pain medication (such as codeine)—can also cause an addiction. Caffeine, found in coffee, tea, and soft drinks, is a highly addictive substance, as is nicotine in cigarettes. Foods can also be addictive, either physically or psychologically.

A process addiction is similar to a chemical addiction, except that you are addicted to a behavior. One very common process addiction is workaholism. The workaholic is addicted to work. All you do is think about work, you can't wait to get there, and you have trouble leaving. Like a chemical addiction, there are both a psychological and physical aspect of the addiction. Psychologically, you are always thinking about work and can't get it out of your mind. You may also get a physical adrenaline high from working constantly. Since you are working so hard, your body adjusts to high levels of stress, so when you begin to cut back you may notice a significant drop in physical energy. This may be followed by depressed feelings. In order to fight this change in energy and feelings you will get back into your addiction. Other process addictions include sex, gambling, overeating, relationships, and even exercise.

The Stages of Chemical Use

Chemical dependency is a progressive disease with particular characteristics that develop over time. The following model can be used to describe the addiction process to any mood-altering chemical(s):

Experimentation>>Moderate Use>>Abuse>>Dependency>> Death>>

When you use any mood-altering chemical for the first time it is called *experimental use*. After such use you decide, either consciously or unconsciously, that you either want to continue or that you don't want to try it again. If you do decide to use it again you quickly move into the second stage of the process, *moderate use*.

During moderate use, your use patterns are fairly predictable. You may use on weekends, in social settings, or with dinner. The amount of chemicals used will vary from time to time. Most important, there are likely to be few consequences directly related to your use. Your work life and relationships are not directly affected by use of the substance. If there is a consequence as a result of your use, in this stage you will be able to recognize that you need to make a change in your using behavior to avoid additional consequences.

For example, Tony was psychologically abused by his alcoholic father. As a result he became very reluctant to drink or use other drugs because of his fear of being genetically predisposed to alcoholism. However, on occasion he would indulge by drinking a glass of wine in a social setting. One night he drank more than usual and as a result became fairly intoxicated. He became verbally abusive toward the host and knocked over a vase. The next morning he felt very remorseful and called the host to apologize for his behavior. He had never gotten drunk before, and his experience made him realize that he couldn't tolerate more than one glass of wine. He decided to curb his drinking for a while and has never had a similar incident. That was ten years ago.

Tony could easily have crossed over the line from moderate use to *abuse* had he not acknowledged the relationship between his behavior and his drinking. The main difference between moderate use and abuse is denial. If you are an abuser you deny any relationship between your problems and your use. The consequences of your use begin to increase in seriousness and frequency, but you use rationalizations, excuses, and blaming whenever these problems occur, and subsequently you are unable to connect the consequences with your use. As an abuser you also have difficulty seeing how your use affects those around you, so you don't try to alter your use in spite of the concerns of family members, friends, or coworkers. Over time your use may increase in frequency and amount and problems begin to develop in all areas of your life. Interpersonal and work relationships may show signs of stress, and serious problems may arise. You may begin to get in trouble with the law. Your previous patterns of work and home life may change for the worse. Your health may begin to deteriorate.

The line between abuse and *dependency* is different for each person. When you become dependent, either physically or psychologically, your life becomes unmanageable. Consequences will show up in all areas—personal, family, and work. When you become dependent your life begins to revolve around your chemical use. You frequently think about using or participating in activities associated with using. Your use is out of control. You either can't stop using once you begin, or you are unable to follow through with promises to cut down or stop altogether. Most important, you continue to use in spite of the adverse consequences associated with use. You may need to use every day in order to avoid severe withdrawal symptoms. Or you may have a pattern of periodic binging separated by a few days, weeks, or months of no or low use. You may appear to have it together, but people close to you will become increasingly aware of how the addiction is affecting your life.

As use progresses you may do severe, irreversible physical damage to the body. Withdrawal symptoms may be difficult because of extreme DTs (delirium tremens), headaches, anxiety, depression, hallucinations, chills, and hot flashes. If you continue to use you will reach the final stage of chemical dependency: *death*. This may occur as a result of an overdose, of mixing chemicals, of complete physical deterioration, or of getting into an accident while intoxicated.

Your using pattern develops after that first experimental use. The length of time it takes you to reach the end of the process will vary. You may use chemicals for years before becoming chemically dependent, or you may show signs of chemical dependency right from the first experience. If you have a family history of alcoholism or drug addiction, you may be genetically predisposed to some forms of chemical dependency. This predisposition may cause the progression of the disease to occur more quickly.

What Role Do Chemicals Play in Your Life?

Ask yourself the following questions:

- How has your chemical use affected your life?

- How has it affected those around you?

- What effects has it had on your emotions, health, and behavior?

- What affects has it had on your family?

For example:

- Last week I got arrested for drunk driving. It was the second time, and it looks like I'm going to lose my driver's license.

- I use alcohol and pot. It helps me relax at the end of the day. When I get high, I guess I do space out a little and I'm not much good to talk to. Come to think of it, I don't get to spend much quality time with my son. He and I are not as close as we used to be.

- I am gaining weight from too much drinking. I have a high-stress job and my doctor told me that I was at high risk for heart disease, but I could do a lot to prevent it by stopping drinking.

- My wife and I fight a lot after I have had too much to drink. On a few occasions I've hit her. She's talking about divorce. That's why I went into counseling.

Process Addictions

The stages of chemical use can also be applied to process addictions. Instead of using a chemical, you have an out-of-control behavior that is causing you severe personal problems. Let's take one common addiction of wounded men: workaholism.

Your first day on the job signals the experimental stage. Once you decide to continue in the job the moderate stage begins. Typically you work from nine to five; occasionally, however, you may need to work longer hours. You may put in excessive hours and be less effective the next day, physically or mentally exhausted, or even physically ill. A family member may voice concern and bring this to your attention. If you are not addicted to work, you will see the relationship between your personal, physical, or family problem and the work schedule and make the necessary adjustments; if that's not possible you will consider changing jobs altogether.

When you continue to work long and hard hours—in spite of the effects it may have on you personally or physically—you are beginning to develop abusive patterns. To justify your behaviors you will use denial in the form of rationalizations ("It's only during the holiday season"), excuses ("I can only work after everyone leaves at night"), explanations ("I had to get this report out"), and blaming ("My boss forced me to do it"). You will tend not to connect your poor health or problems at home with the job. You may work to avoid the problems at home, or may even become depressed if you slow down or take a break. Over time you work harder and harder and the negative consequences in your life become more and more serious and frequent.

When you become dependent, negative consequences are beginning to show up in all areas of your life: at home, emotionally, physically, with friends and family, and possibly even at work. Your life revolves around your work. You think about work constantly. You can't get away from it. Your marriage may be falling apart. You probably don't have a relationship with your children. You may not have any friendships outside of your job. Your physical health may be deteriorating. Yet, in spite of these consequences, you continue to work excessively. You may try to cut back, but after a short time you continue to overload your work life.

What Role Do Process Addictions Play in Your Life?

Ask yourself the following questions:

- What addictive process patterns can you identify in your life?

- What effects have they had on your emotions, health, or behavior?

- What effect have they had on your family?

For example:

- I think I am addicted to sex. It helps me relax. I think about it a lot. I spend a lot of money on magazines and I am constantly hitting on women.

- I have had VD a couple of times. I worry about AIDS. It's difficult for me to have a long-term relationship. I'm lonely most of the time.

- I don't have a family. I wish I did.

There are four potential problems to developing an addiction of any kind.

Any Addiction Is a Serious Problem

First, you will never heal the wound that's causing the pain and anguish if you are using medication or indulging in an activity obsessively to hide the symptoms. Chemical and process addictions do just that. They keep your level of tolerance for psychic pain high enough so that you don't have to deal with the brokenness inside.

Second, addictions are detrimental to your health. Chemical use clearly hurts your body, but process addictions can also have a negative effect on your health. Workaholism can lead to physical stress, and that can lead to physical illness. Overeating can lead to obesity. Gambling can lead to bankruptcy or arrest and consequent lack of income, another stress producer.

Third, any addiction can have a potentially lethal effect on you and the people around you. Death from alcohol and other drugs is the most blatant example, but it is not unusual for men in their early thirties to experience heart disease as a result of overworking With the advent of AIDS and other serious sexually communicable diseases, some individuals who are sexually promiscuous may be risking their lives by utilizing unsafe sex practices. Violence in the family is also highly correlated with both process and chemical addictions.

Fourth, there is mounting evidence that addictions are passed down from generation to generation. Certain types of chemical dependency have a genetic component. If you are addicted to alcohol, for example, you may pass on that tendency to your children. Aside from the genetic link, however, children who grow up in addictive families learn addictive behavior and are psychologically prone to develop similar problems when they become adults.

The choice of the addict is to live or to die. If you are addicted to either a substance or a process, your death may be symbolic (in that you have died emotionally, intellectually, or spiritually) or your death may be literal. On the other hand, living means being heroic

Life or Death?

Chemical Addiction Treatment

If you have an alcohol or drug problem you can find help just about anywhere. The yellow pages have listings under Alcoholism Information and Treatment Centers or Drug Abuse and Addiction Information and Treatment Centers. Alcoholics Anonymous is also listed in the white pages. There are inpatient and outpatient programs for this problem. If chemicals are a problem in your life, you will need to deal with it if you expect to heal from childhood abuse. Get an assessment by a qualified chemical-dependency counselor and get treatment if it's recommended.

Twelve Step Programs

Although talking to professionals can be very helpful in addressing your problem, it can be equally helpful to talk with someone who has already been where you have and can tell you what you can expect in the days ahead. The best-known self-help programs are Alcoholics Anonymous (AA) and Narcotics Anonymous (NA). These programs exist in practically every city around the world, day and night. Although going to a meeting may seem difficult, inconvenient, and awkward, it is important to develop the necessary support to help you address your addiction. At the same time you will establish contacts, so if you have the urge to go back to your old habits you know where and to whom you can go for support.

Al-Anon meetings are for family and friends of alcoholics to learn to recognize ways in which they enable, or inadvertently encourage, an addict to use. Co-dependency groups are similar to Al-Anon, in that they help persons examine dysfunctional ways of solving problems. ACoA meetings are for adult children of alcoholics. CoA meetings are for children of alcoholics. All of these problems use the Twelve Steps developed by AA and NA to help friends and family members recover from addictive family dynamics that serve to promote the problem of addiction rather than solve it.

If you attend any of these groups, you will find that asking for a sponsor can help you through the early stages of recovery. A sponsor is a person who is already well into his or her own recovery. Your sponsor is a person to call when you feel the urge to use or act out in other ways. He is someone with whom you can discuss your difficulties and successes during your recovery. He is someone who has experienced many of the same emotions you are feeling. He has walked and is still walking the same path as you. Most importantly, he is someone who has worked and is still working the steps to recovery.

The Twelve Steps of AA and NA are the key to sobriety. They are rules for healthy and positive living. The Twelve Steps can help any person who is trying to overcome personal difficulties. Twelve Step programs advocate seeking the help of a higher power because people with addictions are notorious for wanting to do things their way. This is called self-willing: "I can do it myself; I don't need any help." It is important for anyone with an addiction to be able to turn to a higher power that will help them overcome their addictive impulses. Their higher power is a greater force that will remind them of what they need to do to stay sober. Aside from the spiritual aspect of the Twelve Steps, following them will improve a person's life in many ways. When men ask, "How can I get sober or recover from my addiction?" the answer is in the letters of the word *HOW*: honesty, openness, and willingness. You need to be honest with yourself and others. You need to be open to the Twelve Steps and the AA/NA fellowship, and you need to be willing to go to all lengths to get sober and heal. That's how AA/NA works.

The Twelve Steps of Alcoholics Anonymous*

1. We admitted we were powerless over alcohol—that our lives had become unmanageable.
2. Came to believe that a Power greater than ourselves could restore us to sanity.
3. Made a decision to turn our will and our lives over to the care of God as we understood Him.
4. Made a searching and fearless moral inventory of ourselves.
5. Admitted to God, to ourselves, and to another human being the exact nature of our wrongs.
6. Were entirely ready to have God remove all these defects of character.
7. Humbly asked him to remove our shortcomings.
8. Made a list of all the persons we have harmed, and became willing to make amends to them all.
9. Made direct amends to such people wherever possible, except when to do so would injure them or others.
10. Continued to take personal inventory and when we were wrong promptly admitted it.
11. Sought through prayer and meditation to improve our conscious contract with God as we understood Him, praying only for knowledge of His will for us and the power to carry that out.
12. Having had a spiritual awakening as the result of these Steps, we tried to carry this message to alcoholics, and to practice these principles in all our affairs.

*The Twelve Steps are taken from Alcoholics Anonymous (New York: Alcoholics Anonymous World Services, 1960), 59–60.

and doing battle with your inner demons. It also means struggling to become a better person, getting to know yourself better, and developing social living skills so that you are more prepared to cope with the curveballs life throws you. Being alive means feeling your pain, but it also means feeling your joy. It means that you will ultimately feel better about yourself and those around you. It will lead to a greater ability to love, be loved, and have peace of mind. Being alive is knowing that you are doing the best you can in an imperfect world.

Stopping Addictive Patterns

The first step in stopping the cycle of addiction is to break denial. It is important to acknowledge that you are developing or do have an addictive pattern. The next step involves getting help. You have probably been trying to deal with your addiction alone, but you won't get anywhere without the help of others.

How do you find out if you are or are becoming chemically dependent? Get an assessment from a qualified chemical-dependency counselor. For process addictions you will find counselors and groups that specifically deal with your type of addiction, such as overeaters groups, sex-addicts, etc. See Chapter 11 for suggestions as to where you can get help.

Get Help!

This recommendation cannot be underscored enough. Although the advice in this chapter sounds easy and straightforward, developing an intellectual understanding of what needs to be done is not enough to break old patterns. Every wounded man can benefit from counseling. When your wounds begin to affect your behavior to the extent that the safety of others is being compromised you must take immediate action to control yourself. This means that you need counseling now! Don't waste any time. The longer you wait, the more likely it is that your problem will get worse. If violence or addiction is a problem in your life, go immediately to the Appendix to get information on how to find counseling. Remember, your recovery is in your hands.

Chapter 8

HEALING THROUGH SEXUALITY

Sexuality is a very important issue for all wounded men to address. Like attitudes about self-esteem and trust, sexual attitudes are formed early in childhood. Abuse has probably affected your feelings and attitudes about sex, which in turn may determine your sexual behaviors. There is a high correlation between abuse as a child, especially sexual abuse, and adult sexual violence and dysfunction. Therefore it is critical that this issue be explored during your healing journey.

How Sexual Attitudes Are Formed

The outcome of your feelings and attitudes largely depends on the overt and subtle messages you received from your family. If sex was considered a dirty word in your family, you may have developed negative associations with sexuality; if sex was talked about openly, without negative judgments, then you may have developed a positive attitude as an adult. Likewise, if sex was used to control and dominate others in your family, then that attitude was probably transmitted to you.

Your first experience with sex may also greatly affect your feelings and attitudes. If you were a victim of sexual abuse you may have come to believe either that sex between an adult and a young person is appropriate or that sex is bad or dirty. You may avoid sex altogether because of negative memories or associations that interfere with your concentration. You may feel uncomfortable with certain types of touch with your partner. You may also have been conditioned to believe that sex is an appropriate outlet for pent-up feelings of rage, sadness, or inadequacy.

Men tend to have very different feelings, attitudes, and expectations about sex than women do, which can complicate the healing process for a wounded man in a relationship. Men often sexualize their feelings and as a result view sex as their primary means of feeling intimate with a woman, whereas women often look to talking, spending time together, and relating as a way of expressing feelings, which may or may not lead to becoming sexually intimate. Men also receive many messages throughout their lives that reinforce the belief that much of their manhood depends on sexual functioning.

A man who was sexually abused as a child received the additional message that sex is a way of managing stress and anxiety and maintaining control over others. The adult victim of sexual abuse is at high risk for acting out these patterns with young children or with adult women or men. Therefore developing new patterns of dealing with stress, anxiety, and the need to be in control are necessary to breaking the generational cycle of abuse.

Everyone would like to be able to associate sexual intimacy with only positive feelings *all* the time. Unfortunately this is just not the case. In reality most people have periodic sexual experiences that are less than enjoyable. For example, how many times have you not been in the mood but agreed to having sex anyway? The result was probably a less than perfect experience. What about times you were tired or not feeling well? What about when you were preoccupied with work or money problems? These are occasional problems we all experience, and we usually don't worry about them.

Many wounded men are generally not satisfied with their sexual experiences. During sex they may be feeling angry, frightened, or confused. They may also have trouble feeling physically or emotionally turned on. Many of these individuals may be psychologically reexperiencing traumatic experiences from their past, which is affecting their sexual feelings today.

What are your feelings about your sexuality? Do you feel angry, sad, or confused during sex? Do you find sexual intimacy threatening, an invasion of your personal space? Do you have difficulty feeling physical sexual sensations or distinguishing when you are turned on and when you don't want sex? Do you avoid sex in order to avoid your feelings? Is having sex a way of avoiding your feelings? Do you have sexual urges or fantasies that you fear are "not normal"? Have you felt sexual feelings toward children? Have you forced people to have sex with you? If you relate to one or a number of these difficult feelings and behaviors about sex you are not alone. What's more, there are specific steps you can take to deal with these and other sexual problems.

I've heard it said that "feelings are like savings bonds: The longer you keep them, the more they mature." Stuffing painful feelings about sex will only make it more difficult for you to address the particular sexual problem you are experiencing. Just as you broke denial about your childhood abuse, you need to admit the sexual problem to yourself and eventually to your partner. Breaking the

Sexual Feelings: The Good, the Bad, and the Confusing

The First Step: Talk about Your Thoughts and Feelings

silence will feel like a weight off your shoulders. Don't forget to let the person in whom you confide know what you want from them in terms of support, just listening, advice, and so on.

If you have a supportive partner, this person may be the one you confide in. If you fear that person won't understand or if you are not in a relationship with someone with whom you have established that level of communication, you may want to talk with a close friend, relative, or counselor.

Step Two: Look at How These Feelings May Relate to Your Abuse

If you were sexually abused as a child, chances are you are experiencing problems directly related to your victimization. You may be feeling afraid of having sex for fear of thinking about or remembering your own abuse. Or you may be having compulsive sex with multiple partners to avoid feelings that can cause pain in others and also be self-destructive. You may have learned from observing your abuser that sex can be a way to avoid personal problems.

Many men and women abused as children have learned to shut off physical feelings of pleasure altogether. This may have begun when you were a child in an effort to feel less physical pain from physical or sexual abuse. But you cannot turn off bodily sensations in order to avoid physical pain without shutting down to physical pleasure as well.

Like physical violence, sexual violence can be a way of exercising control over others without regard for their feelings and well-being. Controlling sexual urges may be more difficult than controlling urges to hit someone. In our society there are still many overt and covert messages that dominating women is a sign of masculinity and success. As with physical violence, men who are sexually abusive need the structure of a counseling program to learn the skills necessary to control their urges and solve personal problems in a more constructive manner.

These are only a few ways that your feelings about sex may be related to your childhood abuse. Making the connections between now and then can help you understand your feelings so you are less likely to think you are crazy for having the feelings in the first place. Don't forget: Uncomfortable sexual feelings are a common outcome of childhood abuse.

I know that reaching out for help is not in our program as men. Our fears that others will perceive us as being inadequate or weak often get in the way of our getting the support and assistance that we need to solve our problems. But these types of problems rarely go away on their own. In fact, they usually get worse if we avoid them. Therefore it is crucial that you seek help from a qualified counselor who is skilled in the area of treatment of child sexual abuse or sexual offenders.

Step Three: Get Help!

Sexual-desire problems relate to one's appetite for sex. Sexual-desire problems are common for men who were abused as children. Unresolved feelings may cause intrusive thoughts, flashbacks, and memories to occur during sexual experiences. You may have found yourself avoiding sex altogether in order to escape such thoughts. It is not unusual for some men to go in the opposite direction and become hypersexual or sexually addictive (compulsive sexual behavior), focusing only on the physical experience and remaining detached from any emotional involvement.

Sexual Problems: Desire Problems versus Dysfunctions

It is also not unusual for men who were abused as children to either become prostitutes or frequent them for sexual satisfaction. Pornography addictions are not uncommon for wounded men. Sexual-identity problems—that is, "Am I gay, straight, or bisexual?"—may also be a concern for you. Any of these can be a problem, because of the high health risk to you and your partners, legal risks, and the devastating psychological and emotional effects for you and your family.

Sexual dysfunction can also be related to childhood abuse. A sexual dysfunction is when something doesn't work the way it should. The most common forms of sexual dysfunction with men are premature ejaculation (ejaculating before you *want* to ejaculate) and erection problems (impotence, inability to get or maintain an erection).

If any of these sexual issues are present in your life and causing you concern, addressing them directly can be an important part of your healing journey.

Lack of Sexual Desire   You can lack sexual desire for any one of a number of reasons. You may discover that during sexual activity you find yourself thinking about the acts of abuse. Or you may find yourself feeling angry, sad, or frightened for no apparent reason during sex. You may feel uncomfortable having sex because you believe that it is bad or that you're dirty for feeling sexual.

You may go about avoiding sex in any one of a variety of ways. Perhaps you simply tell your partner that you are not interested. Maybe you avoid relationships altogether. Having sex with prostitutes may help you avoid the discomfort of sex with your partner.

Leonard worked the graveyard shift and his wife worked days. Although she tried to convince him to change shifts, he argued that the money was better during that time. On weekends he would either go hunting, fishing, or attend football or baseball games. He and his wife led separate lives. He came into therapy after being arrested for hitting her during an argument. This particular argument was sparked by a discussion about sex. Evelyn was feeling frustrated from their lack of sexual contact. Leonard protested her complaints, accusing her of not being supportive of his work. After a number of sessions he disclosed that he had been sexually abused by his stepfather. His father had also avoided the family and, as a result, his mother left him for another man. His stepfather would come into his room in the middle of the night and fondle him. His stepfather had sodomized Leonard by the time he was twelve years old.

As Leonard got older he was very uncomfortable when women made sexual advances toward him. His first marriage ended because of sexual problems. He rationalized to himself, The way to avoid another marriage's failing is to avoid having sex. What better way but to work when she sleeps? Leonard had never told his current wife about the abuse.

After a while Leonard began to realize how much he had tried to avoid those memories and his feelings altogether. That's why he would feel angry at his wife when she confronted him about sex. The first step for him was to talk about the abuse with his therapist—someone whom he viewed as safe—who wasn't going to think that he was crazy. The next step was to talk with his wife about the abuse and why he was avoiding being intimate with her. Then in therapy, they began to discuss how they could begin to reinitiate sexual contact with each other.

LEONARD: I know that I'm not very comfortable with sex because of the abuse with my stepfather. I don't think I ever learned how to ask a woman for sex. I never learned to say no either. I would just run away or avoid situations where I would have to deal with it. Anyhow, I guess I want you to go slowly. I need to know that I can say no. It scares me to think I may be a lousy lover. So is it okay with you to do this?

EVELYN: Sure, are you kidding? I'll do anything to get us back together. I don't understand why you never told me about this. I wasn't going to hate you.

LEONARD: I wasn't worried about you hating me as much as thinking I was weird or crazy.

EVELYN: I don't think you're crazy. What can I do to make you feel good again about sex?

THERAPIST: He'll need to do it, not you.

LEONARD: We've been talking about this in my sessions. I guess I need to begin talking with you about my needs—whatever those are.

EVELYN: Okay. Tell me what you like.

LEONARD: What I like? I don't know what I like.

THERAPIST: That's a good place to start. All people know what they like, they just don't usually think about it. Are you willing to do an exercise?

How Can You Communicate Your Sexual Needs?

(The exercises in this chapter are not intended to replace professional counseling. If sexual problems are occurring in your relationship, help is available.)

It takes a great deal of patience and understanding to overcome barriers to sexual enjoyment. Talking about sexual likes and dislikes is one step in the right direction. Every couple has problems communicating sexual likes and dislikes, but most of your problems in the sexual arena can be solved through communication. Make a time to sit down by yourself or with your partner to discuss your sexual likes and dislikes. Find out what your partner likes and dislikes. (If you find this exercise too threatening to do with your partner, that's okay. Do it by yourself, with a friend, or a counselor.)

What kinds of things turn you on? What turns you off? Write down or discuss your likes and dislikes about making love. Be specific. What kinds of clothes, hair, body types, or smells get you sexually aroused? What type of touch do you like? What type of touch do you find uncomfortable? How do you like to make love? What positions do you prefer? How do you like to touch others and how do you like to be touched? Do you like to talk during sex or listen to music? Do you like to share or listen to fantasies? Do you like to make love in the dark or in the light? During the day or night? Do you like to give massages or get massages? Do you like to get yourself undressed or be undressed by your partner? Do you like to talk before or after making love? The questions are endless.

If you do this exercise with your partner, listen to each other's likes and dislikes without responding. Although you will be tempted to talk about your similarities and differences, this is an opportunity simply to learn about each other, not to negotiate new rules. If you are uncertain about what makes you feel good, experiment (either alone or with your partner) with various types of touch on different parts of your body.

Some men use hypersexuality or compulsive sexuality to avoid uncomfortable feelings about their abuse. Hypersexuality or compulsive sexuality is the desire to have frequent sex without much emotional contact. This type of behavior is sometimes referred to as "sexual addition." This can be acted out with one partner or with multiple partners. Sex becomes a way of venting strong feelings, many of which may be stemming from the abuse, without dealing with them directly; it becomes an outlet for your anger and pain.

Because of social conditioning most men find it easier to separate feelings from the physical act of sex. As a wounded man you may be particularly prone to dissociate from your feelings in intimate relationships because, as you grew up, *not feeling* was a key to your survival. As a result you can be sexual without experiencing emotions. The physical sensations become the entire focus of sex. These sensations can be quite addictive and, as with chemical addictions, over time, you may become sexually compulsive. In addition to the obvious problems of never getting close to another person and not dealing with the underlying problem of abuse, today this type of behavior has high health risks associated with it, both for you and your partners.

Bret describes how sex became a safe way of feeling close without feeling frightened:

> I was very sexually active in college. I never associated it with the abuse, but I now know why I liked it so much. I could be close to someone without their knowing much about me. I didn't want them too close, because I knew they would hurt me in some way like my father did. I used to love having sex and lying together in bed afterwards. I felt so close to another human being. But the minute she became demanding of something more I would get up and leave. I would dread waking up in the morning and having her say something like, "Can I see you again?" I would experience that moment as an intrusion. Like when my father would fuck me. I didn't want to get that close to anyone, never!

**Hypersexuality/
Compulsive
Sexuality**

Mark didn't identify himself as having a sexual problem until he realized that he couldn't make a lasting commitment to a woman. He enjoyed romancing women and, as he put it, "the conquest" of having sexual relations. He enjoyed sex so much that whenever he felt uncomfortable with his life he'd find a woman and get into bed with her. The women he chose to conquer were often vulnerable or seriously looking for a committed relationship. Inevitably, he would break up with them abruptly, leaving them crying or angry. Sex and romance became a way to express his hostile feelings toward women (especially his mother, who didn't stop his father from abusing him) and in the process avoid true intimacy.

Whenever I was bored, lonely, or depressed I would call up one of the many women I knew and set up a date to get together. It would inevitably lead to sex. Afterward I would feel afraid of their wanting a relationship with me so I would leave as soon as possible. I cared for these women. I just didn't want to spend any time with them other than a short date and sex. This was great until I turned forty-eight. I realized that I had never been really close with one person. None of these women I had been with knew me. I felt so alone. Just how I felt growing up.

Prostitution and Pornography

A large percentage of men and women who become prostitutes were sexually abused as children. They may have learned as children that they can get what they want in the world (for example, money and possessions) through sex.

It is also common for men who were abused as children to frequent prostitutes. Sex with a prostitute is less complicated than sex with an intimate. It is straightforward and usually directed toward only one person's pleasure. You can divorce yourself from all emotions and live out your sexual fantasies in an anonymous environment. Some prostitutes will perform sexual acts your partner won't allow.

All these may be reasonable justifications for frequenting a prostitute, but there is a down side. An unfortunate element of prostitution is that you will be receiving pleasure at the expense of someone else. Prostitution is degrading of women and yourself. It is illegal. Many prostitutes work for a pimp who either physically or sexually abuses them. Their work as prostitutes may be their only way to act out their own inner pain as a result of being physically or sexually abused as children. In this way you may be contributing to your own and unintentionally contributing to someone else's cycle of violence. Prostitutes put themselves in great danger of being assaulted by a customer and both run the risk of contracting communicable diseases.

If you frequent prostitutes or if you are working as one, you need to examine your motivations, feelings, and thoughts about your actions. You need to ask yourself, Are my actions hindering or helping my healing process? This is a difficult question to answer and therefore will take much reflection. I am not placing a judgment on you if you either become or frequent a prostitute. I do, however, advise you to look inside and see if your actions are at all related to your being a wounded man. Are you trying to work out the abuse in a way that seems only to reinforce negative coping patterns?

For example, it may be easier for you to have sex without feeling or if you feel you are in charge of another person, but is this really what you need to reinforce in yourself in the long run? If your behaviors are related to your childhood abuse, then for healing to occur you need to deal with your inner pain in a more productive way. You may not be able to answer these questions by yourself. Talking with a trusted friend, partner, or therapist can help you get clear as to how your behavior is affecting you inside and whether or not it's ultimately helpful or destructive.

Like prostitution, pornography can be a way of dealing with your own inner pain of childhood abuse. But pornography, especially violent pornography, is degrading to women, men, and children and serves only to reinforce social stereotypes about men, women, and sexuality. Additionally, developing an addiction to pornography, like any addiction, transforms emotional energy into destructive behavior patterns that reinforce themselves. The more you do it the better you feel—so you keep doing it. Pornography can be a way of avoiding real people and forming intimate relationships. Meanwhile, the healing process from childhood abuse neither progresses nor improves. Once again, you need to confront this issue and you need to ask yourself, Are my actions hindering or helping my healing process?

Sexual-Life-style Confusion

One possible outcome of childhood abuse is confusion about adult sexual life-style choices. This concern is so common because the majority of men were sexually abused by men. If this was true for you, you may have secretly wondered to yourself as you were growing up, Am I a homosexual? or Do men find something about me attractive? If you have been unable to answer these questions, you may find yourself acting out your conflicts rather than facing them. For example, if you are fearful that you may be homosexual or attractive to gay men, you may become hypersexual or promiscuous with women in order to prove your virility to yourself and others. Or you may avoid sex altogether. Men's homophobia or fear of being labeled a "sissy" or "less than a man" interferes with their looking at these issues altogether. As a result they never change archaic attitudes, judgments, and fears about homosexuality and subsequently cling to sexual stereotypes that limit their image of what it means to be a man.

One way to address this issue involves understanding the difference between sexual fantasies and sexual life-style. It is not unusual for men, abused or not, to have fantasies about having sex with other men. And these fantasies are a problem only if they interfere with your sexual pleasure.

Sam was physically abused as a child. He came into one of our sessions wondering if it was normal to have fantasies about having sex with men. I explained to him that any fantasy was "normal" as long as it didn't stop him from enjoying his sexual experiences. In other words, it was okay for him to fantasize about having sex with one or twenty men (or one or twenty other women, for that matter). Barry, on the other hand, would have fantasies about men while having sex with his partner. He would often have erection problems, and as a result frequently avoided having sex. When he had sex with his partner he would frequently become sullen and withdrawn. His fantasies were greatly affecting his sexual enjoyment.

Sexual life-styles—that is, heterosexuality, homosexuality, or bisexuality—is a choice and is not a problem in and of itself. It's only a problem if you are acting out one orientation but for various reasons feel differently inside. It is possible that through the healing process you may come to question your sexual life-style and that you may either change that orientation or eliminate doubts about choices you may have made in the past. The process by which you go about making these decisions will determine how good you ultimately feel about your decision. It is very important that you talk about your questions, confusions, and doubts with a counselor or someone who has already gone through a similar process. As with any important decision, it helps to examine the pros and cons of the various options. Try to be aware of your feelings about each option—all your feelings, positive and negative. Although you may feel as if you are the first or only person who has ever asked himself these questions, you are not. There are many support groups and books written for men who question their sexual orientation. Don't do it alone. A counselor, support group, friends, and even a supportive partner can make the process of understanding yourself a lot easier. And finally, as with any problem, take your time and be patient with yourself.

Sexual Dysfunctions: Premature Ejaculation and Erection Problems

Premature Ejaculation

Premature ejaculation is one of the most common forms of sexual dysfunction for all men, wounded or not. Premature ejaculation is when you cannot voluntarily control your ejaculatory process. Typically you will become aroused and quickly ejaculate even though you did not want to quite yet. This problem can be very frustrating to both you and your partner. There is no specific length of time that you should be able to stay erect without reaching orgasm. Ideally you should be able to have an orgasm when you want to. For example, sometimes you may want to prolong lovemaking for hours; sometimes you want to have a quickie. You are premature if you ejaculate before you or your partner wants you to ejaculate. However just because you ejaculate it doesn't necessarily mean that lovemaking has to end. Many times you may have another erection in a short period of time or you can resort to other forms of lovemaking.

Premature ejaculation often occurs when a wounded man is uncomfortable having sex because of feelings, self-judgments, or flashbacks. There are a number of treatments for this problem, and the success rate is very high. In addition to learning techniques for controlling the ejaculatory process, you need to talk about your feelings, thoughts, and flashbacks as well. Techniques won't help unless you are also able to lessen your anxiety associated with sex.

Erection Problems   You may also experience problems getting an erection or maintaining one. *Impotence* is the traditional word used to describe this phenomenon. The problem with this word is that it has many negative associations. You may associate impotence with lack of manliness, power, or strength. Erection problems can be very frustrating for you and your partner, but the difficulty can be easily solved with patience and communication. Let's look at some of the more common reasons why men have erection problems.

Sexuality is directly affected by our thoughts, physiology, attitudes, and feelings. Sometimes it seems as if the penis has a mind of its own. Every man has had the experience of wanting to have intercourse when his penis did not; or of having of "pistol in his pocket" and no thought of sex on his mind.

Not every problem with erections has something to do with how you are feeling and what you think about your sexual partner. The ability to have an erection can be greatly affected by diet, level of fatigue, changes in blood pressure, medication, and drug usage.

Tony was very frustrated by his inability to maintain an erection. When I asked him about his work, I discovered that he worked a minimum of fourteen hours a day, at least six days a week. Tony was in a state of chronic fatigue. It was amazing that he could get even a brief erection. It would be necessary for him to make a drastic change in his work schedule in order to alleviate his erection difficulties. Within six months he was able to get his work life under control and in doing so was also able to get his sexual performance under control.

Rob had recently graduated from a chemical-dependency program. He had been abusing alcohol and cocaine for twenty years. Sex was always an intense experience when he was high on cocaine, but he frequently had problems either getting or maintaining an erection when sober. Rob needed to learn what it was like for him to have sober sex. Although it felt much less intense, over time he was able to learn to enjoy sex without drugs.

Breaking the Cycle of Child Sexual Abuse

If you were sexually abused as a child there is a possibility that you may develop an impulse to act out sexually with a child. The key to preventing this is to talk with others about your fears, fantasies, and impulses. Doing so will lesson the possibility of acting-out. However, this is a situation where family and friends cannot replace the value of seeking professional help.

Many child sexual abusers turn toward children because they feel intimidated by peers. A person who is younger and smaller is easier to manipulate and control than a spouse or lover. If sex is your only outlet for expressing feeling, and you feel intimidated or afraid of your spouse or another adult, you may find it easier to express your feelings with a child. If you were sexually abused as a child and are afraid of acting out toward your own or other children, it is important for you to get help. By working through your own experiences with abuse and learning how to express your feelings, get your needs met, and feel in control of your life, you will certainly feel less of a need to turn toward others who, by nature of their size and intelligence, are able to make you feel more powerful and in control.

Evan was in counseling for sexually abusing his eight-year-old next-door neighbor. He talked about his own victimization and difficult dealing with his feelings led him to abuse someone else:

> My stepfather used to beat up my mother and then afterward he would go out and get drunk. In the middle of the night she would sneak into my room and sleep with me. Sometimes she'd put her hand under the sheets and start playing with me. Finally, I got old enough to start running away from home and using drugs. I was shy and not able to make girlfriends. I used to baby-sit for my next-door neighbor. We used to wrestle with each other. One thing led to another and I started touching her down there. I was doing to her what my mother did to me but I just didn't realize it. I couldn't confront my mother with my feelings so I turned to this kid. Luckily this all came out into the open. Otherwise I would still be abusing someone else rather than talking about my problems.

Dealing With Sexual Attraction and Impulses toward Children

We are all sexual beings, and it is not unusual for adults to feel sexual attractions toward children. It is also not unusual for children to feel that way toward adults. However, it is a problem if an adult or a child acts on those feelings. We as a society have agreed that sex between adults, especially parents (or stepparents), and children is morally wrong because it causes great psychological and physical damage to the developing child.

Many sex offenders claim that their victim was seductive. Any child can be seen as seductive if you want to see him or her that way. This is not an excuse for acting on your sexual impulses. If a child is seductive, he or she may have learned to be that way to get something from an adult. Many children learn seductive behaviors from other children, television, or movies. It is very important that adults learn to control their impulses and not act upon their fantasies. Doing so will only cause destruction to others. Even though a child may seem cooperative or actually to enjoy the sexual activity, the damage will occur inside just the same and find its way to the surface years later.

Incest Survivors Anonymous (ISA) is a Twelve Step program, similar to Alcoholics Anonymous, for persons sexually abused as children. They utilize the Twelve Steps, identical to AA and NA, to help men and women heal their inner wounds stemming from sexual abuse. They are a self-help program with meetings throughout the United States. Through mutual support members learn how to apply the Twelve Steps to daily living, receive support from other survivors, and have the opportunity to help others learn from their experiences. If a chapter doesn't exist within your area, you can start one by writing or calling ISA headquarters in California (See Resources in Appendix 3).

Preventing sexual abuse is very similar to learning how to control physical or psychological violence. First you have to become aware of the problem in the first place. Then you need to learn to identify and communicate your feelings and needs. Healing from your own victimization experiences is crucial to preventing sexual abuse of children. It is very important that you realize that change can occur. Remember the key attitudes: honesty, openness, and willingness. You need to be honest with yourself and others about what you have done to hurt others. It takes openness to learn new skills and change attitudes toward yourself and others. And finally, it takes a willingness to do whatever it takes to heal. For most men, this includes weekly counseling to learn how to minimize the possibility to acting out these destructive impulses.

Chapter 9

MAKING PEACE
WITH
YOUR ABUSER

At some time in your recovery process you may make the decision that talking with your abuser can actually help the healing process along. There are a number of reasons why you may decide to talk with the abuser:

- Telling your abuser how you felt then and how you feel now is an important part of the disclosure stage.

- Speaking with that person can help you better understand how and why the abuse occurred. If your abuser is receptive to talking about the experience you may be able to get some valuable information to clarify your memory of the events. The abuser who has given his behavior much thought or who has been in therapy can help you understand his or her motivation.

- Speaking with the abuser may alleviate your concerns that others were or are currently being abused.

- You may be interested in establishing a positive and healthy relationship with your abuser.

Confronting the abuser for all or any of these reasons may ultimately help you understand that you were not responsible for the abuse and that the behavior resulted from his or her personal problems, not something inside of you.

You do not *need* to confront your abuser in order to heal from the abuse. Healing from your experiences is a process that occurs inside of you and doesn't necessarily involve the abuser.

If you make the decision to confront your abuser there are a number of issues you may want to think about before acting that can make the experience more productive. First of all you need to plan your initial contact: What do you want to say and what do you expect? You also need to think about that person's possible reactions and how you will respond. What if your abuser is not alive or available? Is it still possible to make peace with that person? And, finally, is forgiveness possible?

Your Initial Contact

Initial contact with the abuser may be very awkward and frightening. Not only will this be uncomfortable for you but the person with whom you will be talking is going to feel equally anxious. Therefore careful planning is important.

There are a number of ways to begin a dialogue with the person who abused you. You can simply sit down with that person and talk about the abuse. This approach may be easy for you if you already have an open line of communication with that person. You may already feel comfortable with your feelings and perceptions about the abuse and your ability to communicate.

But if this issue is too charged for this kind of face-to-face discussion, I would like to suggest other ways to begin preparing for such a dialogue

Writing a Letter   Writing a letter to your abuser can be an excellent way to begin. Whereas a face-to-face conversation can easily escalate into an argument, writing gives both you and the person to whom you are communicating a chance to deliberate before responding. Writing also entails your thinking about your thoughts and feelings. This can be very therapeutic in and of itself. Writing takes the thoughts out of your head and puts them on paper where you can look at yourself in a somewhat detached way. This gives you a different perspective on your experience. You may want to include in your letter what you remember about the abuse, how you felt then, how you feel now, and how the experience affects you today. This is a tall order, so just begin with what comes most naturally. Don't worry initially about how you say, just let the words flow out. You may decide not to send the letter. What is important is that you get the words out of your head and into another form. If you decide to mail it you can send only those parts that you feel most comfortable sending.

John was sexually abused by his uncle. He never told anyone until he was thirty-four years old. One month after he disclosed the abuse to his therapist, he decided to write to his uncle. Here is a portion of that letter.

Dear Uncle Richard,

This is a difficult letter for me to write. We've never talked about what happened between you and me when I was a child. You sexually abused me. There, I said it. You sexually abused me. You know, I have only said that to four people; my brother, my therapist, myself, and now you. I want to tell you how I feel about it. There is so much feeling inside I am not sure how it will come out, but I'm going to try just the same. I want to start off by saying that I have been afraid to write this letter. My therapist has encouraged me for several weeks, so I decided to sit down and give it a try. I am most afraid that you will deny that you sexually abused me. I know it happened. It has taken me twenty years to label it as abuse. I had myself convinced that you were just showing me love and affection. That wasn't love or affection. You used me for your own needs. I know it wasn't for me.

I remember when I would sleep over at your house you would come into my room at night. You began by rubbing my back and then fondling my penis. You would usually masturbate me and one time you tried to have anal sex with me. I remember stopping you because it hurt so much. I would feel so confused. On the one hand it would feel good, and yet on the other hand it would feel very physically uncomfortable and mentally I felt very scared and guilty. I felt as though I was doing something wrong. For twenty years I felt as though I was to blame. I hate you for that. Now I know you are to blame. You knew better, you used me, you abused me!

I am really angry at you. You hurt me. You were part of the reason why I have had so many problems as an adult. Why did you do it to me? You took advantage of me. You knew that I was an unhappy child. You knew that I would do anything for a little love and attention. You betrayed my trust. I feel so much anger inside. I have gone at times between wishing you were dead and wishing I were dead. But as you may recall, I tried that route a long time ago. I don't want to carry the anger and guilt around anymore. It contaminates all my relationships.

I want several things from you at this point. First, I need to know if you are sexually abusing other children now. If so, you need to get help from a professional. I also want to know if you ever got help from a counselor. If so, have you figured out why you did this to me? These problems do not go away by themselves. How do you know you won't do it again? Lastly, I want you to respond to this letter in writing. Right now I don't want to talk with you on the phone or in person. I hope you can understand why I need to deal with this issue. I want to put it behind me but I can only do that by letting you know how I feel. I hope to hear from you soon.

When you write a letter to the person who abused you it is important not to censor any of your thoughts. Put them down on paper as they are in your head. This can be helpful for you because seeing it on paper removes you from the intensity of the feelings. You may even be able to view the experience from another perspective. After John wrote this letter to his uncle, he told me the following:

I couldn't understand why you told me to write it down until I actually wrote the letter. For years I felt guilt and shame about the abuse—so much so, I couldn't talk about it with anyone. But when I wrote the letter I felt different immediately. I really mean it. As soon as I started writing I felt a big relief, as though I were taking a bulldozer load of feelings and dumping them back on him, where they belong.

Speaking into a Tape Recorder

Another way you might begin is by speaking into a tape recorder. Like writing, listening to yourself describe your feelings and thoughts can be an excellent way to view the experience from a different angle. This can also be an opportunity to express feelings that you ordinarily stuff. Don't censor your thoughts or feelings— yell or cry if you need to. Just speak your heart and mind.

Your First Actual Conversation with the Abuser

At some point you may decide to speak with the person directly, either over the phone or in person. Such a discussion could either be greatly rewarding or turn into a disaster. There are ways in which you may want to prepare for and structure the conversation so as to make your chances for success as great as possible.

It is most important to prepare for the discussion. The letter-writing exercise described above can be an excellent way to organize your thoughts prior to the conversation. Think about what points you would like to make in the conversation. For example, you may want to tell the person certain thoughts and feelings. You may also want to know certain information from that person. John outlined his talk ahead of time before he decided to talk with his uncle.

What thoughts I want to tell him:

- He sexually abused me.

- What he did was wrong and illegal.

- I wasn't responsible for his abuse.

- I remember it occurring for three years.

- He masturbated me on many occasions.

- He tried to have anal sex with me but I stopped him.

- I've been in therapy for ten years.

- I told my brother and therapist about the abuse.

- I have been thinking about telling my parents.

- He has a serious problem and he needs to be in counseling.

- His abuse caused me a lot of problems both as a teenager and as an adult.

- He took advantage of my being a lonely kid.

What feelings I want to tell him:

- I am really angry at him.

- He betrayed my trust of him.

- I felt afraid of him when I was a child.

- I thought he only loved me because of my giving him sex.

- I felt used by him.

- Sometimes I wished he were dead.

- Sometimes I wished I were dead.

- I feel so mad that he forced me to do those things.

What I want from him:

- Assurance that he is not abusing other children.

- Who else he has abused.

- What he remembers doing to me.

- Why he did it.

- Did he get help for his problem?

- Does my aunt (his wife) know?

- How does he feel about what he did?

This was quite a lot of information. When John spoke with his uncle for the first time he didn't get to every issue, but it created a good structure for his conversation. During the talk he found out other facts about his uncle and the abuse that he hadn't thought about himself. Fortunately, his uncle was fairly open to the conversation. In fact, he had received some counseling many years ago but still had been afraid to approach the topic with his nephew.

At one point in the conversation his uncle asked John, "What's going to help you get beyond this issue in your life?" John wasn't sure how to answer that question. In fact, John was unable to articulate just what he needed to have happen. He did know, however, that talking about his thoughts and feelings was a major step in the right direction.

The process of healing from childhood abuse is not always a clearly demarcated path, as in reading a map. Sometimes the most direct route from A to point B is not the most productive. Tom's story of talking with his father about his abuse as a child illustrates this point.

Tom's father was psychologically and physically abusive toward Tom. Tom clearly remembers his father's constant criticism and explosions of anger. Tom didn't decide to start off talking about his abusive childhood. Instead he encouraged his father to talk about his own childhood, in particular his relationship with his father. It was through this discussion that Tom began to talk about his memories of his childhood. Rather than confront his father, Tom decided that his father was less likely to get defensive if he were to discuss his memories about childhood in much the same way his father had just done. His father just listened. Suddenly, Tom realized that his father was beginning to cry. For the first time he realized the effect his actions had had on Tom. His father was open to hearing these feelings and thoughts and this conversation began a long series of talks between father and son that has led to a deeper relationship between Tom and his father and has facilitated Tom's healing process.

When the Abuser Minimizes the Abuse

Many abusers are not ready to take responsibility for their abusive behavior. Unless they have closely examined their actions they are likely to have put the abuse out of their minds. For this reason they may act very defensive when you broach the subject of abuse. One such reaction is to minimize the seriousness of their actions or the effects their behavior may have had on you. For example:

Physical abuse:

- "I didn't hit you that hard."

- "You were tough; you didn't seem to mind it."

Sexual abuse:

- "I was just showing you my love and affection."

- "I didn't physically force you to do anything."

Psychological abuse:

- "I didn't mean what I said; I was just angry."

- "You don't remember what I said that long ago."

Minimizing statements, such as these, can be difficult to respond to if you are not prepared. This is why I encourage you to practice talking about the abuse with a close friend, partner, or therapist before you actually confront your abuser. Think about how you would respond to these or similar statements that minimize the seriousness of the abuse or the affects it had on you.

Physical abuse:

- "I didn't hit you that hard."

Your response might be: "I don't think you realize how hard you did hit me. I used to have welts on the back of my legs or I couldn't sit without pain for several hours. Once I bled from being hit with the metal part of a belt. It hurt a lot. You were much bigger and stronger than me. I was afraid of you."

- "You were tough; you didn't seem to mind it."

Your response might be: "I didn't show you how much it did hurt me. If I did you would have laughed at me. You never once asked me if I was all right after a beating. You made me tough, that's how I survived. You don't realize how much you hurt me when you would beat me. I still have dreams about when you would whip me with your belt. You didn't just punish me, you were abusive."

Sexual abuse:

- "I was just showing you my love and affection."

Your response might be: "You sexually abused me. You weren't showing me love, you used me for your own sexual needs. It wasn't mutual, you were in charge and you used your power to get what you want. That wasn't how I wanted to be loved. I wanted you to talk to me, I wanted you to be interested in me. I wanted you to love me for who I was, not for sex. I used to think that the only reason you loved me was because I let you do those things to me. I wanted affection from you, to be held, not to be turned into a sex object."

• "I didn't physically force you to do anything. I wasn't violent."

Your response might be: "I don't think you realize how your mere size and the fact that you were my mother was a form of force. I couldn't say no to you. I was a kid. I wanted your love and approval. You did force me because you never asked me if what you were doing was okay. You tricked and manipulated me. You *were* violent; sexual abuse is violence. You threatened me by telling me not to tell anyone. You were threatening in that you had power over me. You used your power to get what you want. You forced me to do something I didn't want to do."

Psychological abuse:

• "I never laid a hand on you."

Your response might be: "The words you used hurt me a lot longer than physical pain. You were supposed to help me feel good about myself—feel like a valuable human being. Instead you made me feel like a worthless piece of shit and I have been feeling that way for the past twenty years."

• "I was unhappy with my marriage. I didn't mean what I said."

Your response might be: "You might have been unhappy with your marriage but my six-year-old's mind thought it was my fault. I felt so bad all those years because I thought I was the cause of all your problems, and you have to admit, you made me feel that way at times."

Another common response of abusers is to justify their actions.

Like minimizing, this is an attempt to place responsibility for the abuse on the victim or others. For example:

Physical abuse:

- "You were a bad kid."

- "You never listened to what we told you."

Sexual abuse:

- "You were very seductive as a child."

- "Your mother would never have sex with me."

Psychological abuse:

- "You were getting too big for your britches."

- "I did it to build your character."

When you are talking with the person who abused you, do not let them "off the hook." If that person tells you that you were a seductive child, tell him or her, "If I was, I probably learned it from you. That was how I learned to get attention from you," or "That's no excuse." An abuser who minimizes or justifies his actions is challenging you to stand by your beliefs. If you begin to doubt your feelings, question your memory, or became confused, you are once again a victim. As a child you didn't have the choices that you have today. You were dependent on this person and they had power over you just through their size, age, and strength. Today, as an adult, you are on an equal footing with this person. You don't have to be abused anymore. You can express your thoughts and feelings and, above all, you can walk away if you choose.

Denial is an extreme form of minimization and justification. Some abusers will refuse to face their actions no matter how directly they are confronted. When this occurs you have a number of options. No matter what your response, it is important that you recognize your anger—if not to that person, at least to yourself.

You can direct your anger to that person:

- "I am feeling angry that you are denying what happened."

- "I want to stop having contact with you until you can be honest with me."

- "I am feeling very angry with you right now."

- "I want you to come to my counselor with me next week."

You can also tell yourself how you are feeling without expressing those feelings to the other person:

- "I am feeling really angry right now, but I am just going to take a deep breath and keep my cool. I have a list of things I want to say and I am going to get through that list. I am not going to let him get the best of me. If all else fails I can write in my feelings log."

You may also choose to tell the abuser that you don't want to hear his response to you, that you simply want him to listen. In this way you can at least express yourself. Whether or not he chooses to acknowledge your perspective is a separate issue from your being able to ventilate your thoughts and feelings. There is no guarantee that the person will listen calmly. In fact, he may react very defensively, especially if he is afraid of what you are saying to him. If you think that the conversation is getting out of hand, you may choose to end it. You may want to acknowledge that he isn't prepared to hear what you have to say and that perhaps you can talk at another time.

Even if this person denies perpetrating the abuse, it is important

When the Abuser Denies the Abuse

for you to realize that your attempt to confront your abuser can be a valuable experience in and of itself. It takes a great deal of heroism, courage, and self-confidence to talk face to face with your abuser. Doing so can bring all kinds of feelings to the surface that have been long repressed. You may simultaneously feel rage and protectiveness of the abuser. No matter how receptive or unreceptive the abuser is to this discussion, it is grist for the mill in your recovery process.

Talking with Others about the Abuse

Talking with your abuser may be complicated because of your relationship with that person. For example, if the abuser was a parent, should you tell the other parent? If the abuser was a relative or neighbor, should you tell your parents? If not a parent, what about the abuser's spouse and children? Should you talk with your brothers or sisters about the abuse? These are important questions that you may want to spend some time thinking and talking about.

There is a strong argument for not keeping your experience a secret from others in your family. One reason child abuse, in all its forms, exists is because of the veil of secrecy that keeps others from knowing about it. Abusers do not want others to know about their behavior because on some level they realize that what they are doing is wrong. Therefore secrecy is the key to continuing their abusive behaviors. If others were to find out about the abuse, someone would be likely to stop the abuser. Keeping the abuse a secret is one way abusive families become isolated.

Tony talks about how secrecy operated in his family:

We had all kinds of secrets in our family. Of course, no one outside our house knew about the violence. Even our close relatives weren't sure what was going on with us. They probably suspected something, but no one ever said anything to me. We had other kinds of secrets. These mainly had to do with feelings. No one ever talked about feeling angry, sad, unhappy, or anything. The funny thing was that they really weren't secrets. Everyone knew that Mother was depressed and Father was angry, we just didn't talk about it. We also had another secret that related to my brother, Allen. He was using drugs and alcohol, but no one wanted to say anything to him. We would make up excuses of his weird behaviors. We really didn't have any secrets, we all knew what was going on. We just didn't want to face ourselves or each other.

Bret talked about how secrecy only perpetuated the abuse in his family:

He told me not to say anything to anyone about our time together. He told me they wouldn't understand. So I didn't say anything. I know now that had I said something, they would have made him stop abusing me. I kept the secret for almost thirty years. Although I have told my brothers and sister, I still feel like I shouldn't talk about the sexual abuse, that I should keep quiet rather than upset everyone. Everyone would stuff their feelings so as not to upset anyone in our family. Maybe I would have said something then if my parents encouraged us to say what was on our minds. Here I am, a grown man, and I am still afraid to rock the boat.

There is much controversy in the field of child abuse as to what is the best approach to this issue. Some professionals believe that you should talk openly with family members about the abuse. If they don't want to hear about it or deny its occurrence, that is another story. However, it is always better for both the victim and the family to place the issue on the table for everyone to see. This helps to break down the family denial and creates a sense of relief for the victim. Others in the field believe that it is up to the victim to decide who should be told about the abuse. If the victim wants to keep the story to himself, that is his choice. What is important is that he feel that he has complete control in this decision, as opposed to his lack of control over being abused.

Another reason to tell others in the family of the abuse relates to the abuser. This person may have continued to abuse others in your place. If this is the case, you may be in a position to help them avoid further victimization. By telling others of the abuse you experienced and your concern for the safety of others, the abuser may be less likely to act out. In fact, you may want to suggest to the other family members close to that person that they strongly encourage him to get treatment for his problem.

Between telling the world and telling no one there is an in-between position, and that is to tell selected individuals with whom you have a trusting and supportive relationship. There may be one sibling with whom you feel a particular closeness, or an aunt or uncle with whom you can confide. You many want to start with a close friend. No matter whom you choose to tell of the abuse, you are likely to feel as if a load has been taken off your chest. You will no longer be carrying around the secret of your pain and anger. By speaking the truth you have taken an important step in healing the wounds of childhood abuse.

Protecting Your Own Children

If you live near the parent or relative who abused you and that person has minimized or denied the abuse, you may have to evaluate if that person is at risk for abusing your own child. One condition for visiting your children could be their attending counseling sessions with you or on their own. If that person refuses you may have to make the decision to not let your child visit or only under your supervision. This will all depend on your perception of their ability to interact appropriately with your child. Don't make such an important decision alone. Talk with your partner, counselor or other supportive family members.

When the Abuser is Unavailable

In some cases the person who abused you may no longer be available. The person may have died. He might have been a neighbor who moved away. It may be a father, mother, or other relative who long ago broke off contact with the family. Unless you are able to find this person, you will not be able to confront them directly about their abusive behaviors. However, there are other ways to meet this need.

As mentioned earlier, in one of my wounded-men groups I placed a chair in the middle of the circle. I then asked each man to place his abuser in that chair and tell him something he had never told him before. The tension in the group greatly increased because of the men's unspoken feelings. Several men mentioned that their abuser had died several years ago. One man stated that he hadn't talked with his father for thirty years. In each case the men had felt relief simply by verbalizing their feelings. You can do a similar exercise. Place a chair in front of you and mentally sit your abuser in the chair. Write out your thoughts and feelings as described earlier, and talk to that person as if he or she were actually sitting before you. You may want to do this exercise with a therapist or someone else with whom you have a close relationship. The other person could help you if you are uncertain what or how to say what's on your mind.

This exercise will help you let go of some of your intense feelings and express thoughts you have been carrying around with you for many years. You will feel a relief whether the person is actually sitting there or not. In addition to this exercise you may also want to confront the "unavailable" abuser by writing him a letter. No matter who you finally confront the person who abused you, it is important to realize that this experience is primarily for you and secondarily for the other person. This means that you should try not to let the other person's feelings interfere with your need to express yourself. It will be difficult for your abuser to hear what you have to say, but it will be equally difficult, if not more so, for you to muster up the courage to speak what is on your mind. If at any point you think you have had enough or you feel uncomfortable, it is your choice to stop the conversation.

Forgiveness

One of the most difficult issues you may face during the healing process is forgiving your abuser. Forgiveness involves letting go of anger or bitterness toward the abuser for his or her actions. You may ask, "How can I forgive someone who has hurt me in that way?" Forgiveness is not something that you can make happen. If it's going to occur, it will do so over the course of healing.

Reverend Marin Fortune, the founding director of the Center for the Prevention of Sexual and Domestic Violence in Seattle, writes that three steps must be taken before forgiveness is possible: truth telling, accountability, and penance. It is important for you to tell yourself and another person what has happened to you. In telling the truth you will break the veil of secrecy that surrounds childhood abuse and purge yourself of the inner turmoil and self-alienation that accompany the silence.

Once the truth is out the offender must be held accountable for his or her actions. This is one reason it may be very helpful for you to confront your abuser. In this way the perpetrator is given the opportunity to take responsibility for his actions, but he does not always do so. You may find that your abuser is remorseful and wanting to make amends, or you may be faced with denial and minimization. Some abusers will take responsibility only after being arrested or sued by their victims. It is very important for you to realize that even if your abuser never takes responsibility or is never held accountable by society or the family, forgiveness is still possible.

If the abuser is confronted and has indicated remorse for his or her actions, this is not enough for forgiveness to occur. Saying "I am sorry" is not adequate for the pain and suffering they have caused. Along with their remorse or apology there must be an indication that the perpetrator has fundamentally changed or is willing to change his or her behavior so as not to cause similar pain in others. It may be difficult to know if this change has occurred. You may have little contact with this person and have no idea if he or she has changed at all. Here is where you need to use and trust your intuition. If you sense a positive difference about this person, then trust your perceptions. If you sense he or she hasn't changed or has even become worse, then you can trust those perceptions.

People can and do change and grow over time. On the other hand, don't let your desire to forgive and forget blind you to reality. If you have ongoing contact with your abuser at this time in your life, you may be able to observe differences that indicate the remorse is genuine, that change for the positive has occurred. With effort on both sides you and your abuser can rebuild a positive relationship. This takes work, in the form of honesty, support, understanding, and patience.

But what if you do not see the possibility of a good relationship with your abuser? Does it mean that forgiveness is not possible? At some point in the healing journey you will be able to say to yourself, "I have done everything I can do to heal this relationship. I do not have control over my abuser's feelings, attitudes, or behaviors." Here is where you need to realize that his or her illness is denial and that you cannot heal that illness. You can only take care of yourself. You will eventually detach yourself from the unhealthy person, and in doing so, you will be able to let go of your anger and your need to control and punish.

Chapter 10

Making Peace with Yourself

Your healing process does not end when you finish this book. In fact, it's just beginning. Your journey will involve a daily commitment to change unhealthy patterns. Healing from childhood abuse is a lifelong process that begins with a recognition, "I was abused," and leads to a better understanding of yourself and ultimately to greater inner peace. The healing process can be cleansing. Working through the pain, anger, and hurt can give you an indescribable feeling of lightness.

An important part of the healing process involves changing behaviors, such as learning to recognize your feelings and clearly identifying negative patterns of coping with conflict and stress. Ultimately, you will experience not only an outer change but an inner transformation. Returning to old patterns, though tempting, will not be as easy as it was before. This is because you know more now than you did when you started. Once you make an effort to communicate your feelings on Monday, it won't be so easy to forget about them on Tuesday. This experience of inner transformation is the beginning to finding peace within yourself.

Throughout this book I have described the stages of healing and ways to implement each stage of the recovery process. You began by disclosing the abuse; then you learned about the effects of the abuse on your feelings, attitudes, and behaviors; and ultimately you began to develop new attitudes, skills, and ways of coping with these effects as well as the struggles of everyday living. The final stage, transformation, begins the moment you decide to heal. The moment you make this decision you are taking the first steps in healing the inner pain and confusion. This doesn't mean that you will stop falling into potholes. It does mean, however, that you will be able to step out of them quickly.

Inner Balance

One manifestation of the transformation process is better inner balance. You will obtain this balance by developing those parts of your personality that can be useful in healing, relating to others, solving conflict, and generally living a more whole life. One area that I have discussed in this book is the balance between feeling and thinking. But there are other areas as well: independence versus dependence, nurturing versus indifference, passivity versus aggressiveness, impulsive versus deliberating behavior, introversion versus extroversion, courage versus fear, self-sacrifice versus selfishness, domineering versus submissive behavior, rationality versus irrationality, being outspoken versus quiet, being rough-natured versus docile. None of these is positive or negative in itself, and any of them might be appropriate depending on the situation. The balanced person is able to respond in a flexible manner. If you are unbalanced you will respond to all situations from a habitual pattern. For example, if you are typically aggressive, you will always act aggressively—even when it's inappropriate to the situation.

We often enter into relationships seeking balance from others. This is as true for friendships as for love relationships. Thinking men are frequently attracted to feeling individuals: introverts are usually attracted to extroverts: if you are fearful of being dependent on someone you may get involved with someone who pulls for greater commitment.

These differences that attract us to one another are also often the source of conflict and disagreement. However, we can use these differences as opportunities to grow, to learn from each other, and to become more whole. The most classic difference is the thinking man who is attracted to the feeling woman. Much of their conflict results from the fact that they speak different languages. If both can be sensitive to and learn the other's language, then conflicts will be less frequent, less intense, and easier to solve. Through the healing process you have the opportunity to develop untapped parts of your psyche, and in doing so you will become more whole.

This is the nature of the transformation process: letting yourself become whole, allowing yourself to experience the whole range of human potential—the feeling and the thinking, the nurturing and the independent, the ambitious and the lazy, the passive and the active. When you allow yourself to be all that you can be, you are no longer shackled by the chains of "should" and "ought to." You define for yourself how you will be rather than leaving that to society or your family. As you change your expectations of yourself, so will you change your expectations of women and other men and thus allow them to be themselves.

Healing and Spirituality

When we face a crisis in our lives that we can't control, such as the death of a loved one or acknowledging abuse, we often turn toward some higher power for a sense of peace and tranquility amid the chaos and confusion. An integral part of developing inner balance may involve coming to terms with your sense of spirituality.

Spirituality is different from religion. Spirituality relates to the human spirit or soul. It is not the worldly or physical universe, such as your body or material possessions; it is that which relates to the in-

tangible, the unexplainable, the unknown. Whereas religion is an orga-
nized form of worship defined by a group, spirituality is defined by you.

Spirituality is different for everyone. You may feel quite comfortable
affiliating yourself with a formal religion or group, or you may want to
develop a relationship with your higher power in a very personal and
unique way. You may look to a particular spiritual leader for insight
and guidance or find the inspiration within yourself.

The need for spirituality may be a difficult concept for you to
accept, either because you have a very fixed sense of your religious
beliefs or because you find it difficult to believe in a God or higher
power. Until now you may not have had a need for spirituality, but
there is a definite place for it in the healing process.

Your higher power or spirituality can help you in a number of
important ways along your healing journey. First, having a peaceful
place to turn to when you are experiencing strong and seemingly
unending waves of emotion can bring you some serenity. Another way
to use your spirituality during your healing process is by letting
yourself surrender control over the exact nature of the process to a
force greater than you. Although this book lays out a general healing
plan for you, what you actually encounter along the way is unknown
to you or anybody else. Trusting that your higher power will lead you
to the place you need to be and will confront you with situations that
will help you learn an important lesson allows you to worry less about
what is around the corner. If you can trust that someone or something
is watching over you, then you can live for today. This process of
surrendering control can enable you to become more humble and
acknowledge your need for help. Ultimately your sense of spirituality
can help you feel more connected to humankind.

Facing Spirituality at a Time of Crisis

Mark flies quite often in connection with his work. One day, in a
time of extreme crisis, he was forced to rethink his relationship with
God while in a plane, 30,000 feet above the ground:

I was flying on a twin-engine jet. All of a sudden the captain gets
on the intercom and says that one of the engines is on fire and

we are going to make an emergency landing. It was clear that there might be a problem touching down, and we would have to take emergency precautions. Well, the flight attendants helped us prepare for the landing without anyone panicking. When I was bent over with my head down I thought, I hope that there is a God, because if I die I don't want it all just to end. I had this image of walking toward a white light and it being warm, safe, and really peaceful. I felt that if God determined that it was time for me to die there would be nothing I could do about it. I really had to let go because I had no control at this time over whether I was going to die or not. But I knew that if it were my time, He would be there to meet me. I was glad that I got to do the things that I did in my life and I was also happy that I was working on changing myself—healing from the abuse. I was sure that God would forgive me for my mistakes because I was doing something about them.

Well, the story ended on a positive note because the plane didn't crash and I didn't die. But I came out of the experience with a better sense of my relationship to God. That was quite an experience.

Spirituality as a Source of Inner Tranquility

Spirituality can help you find inner tranquility in a time of extreme turmoil. Tom describes how he uses his spirituality:

When I am feeling scared, lost, or just need to put things into perspective, I go out by the beach. I sit and meditate. I think about how wonderful the ocean feels. I'm amazed at its power and beauty. I get the same feeling when I go up to the mountains. I marvel at the sheer beauty of the snow-capped peaks, the rivers and waterfalls. I think to myself, there must be a God, because no mortal could have made this. This helps to calm me down. Even when I can't go to these places physically I can go there in my mind and I still feel calmer, more at ease with myself.

Using your spirituality to heal can be a very powerful experience. Bret was sexually abused by his father for many years. When he began to open up with his partner and in therapy, he began to experience extreme mood swings and a lot of anger and hurt. He would at times feel very frustrated that he was unable to control the intensity of his emotions. The only way he was able to cope during this period was to trust in his belief that he needed to go through these feelings and that his higher power would help him endure the pain of healing. His belief in a loving, accepting higher power allowed him to let his feelings out without self-judgment or the urge to repress his feelings. Many men have told me that it was their belief in a greater plan, a higher power, or God that allowed them to experience their grief and trust that they would survive the pain that seemed so endless and unforgiving.

Spirituality and Relinquishing Control

Trying to control everything in the world around you can become a burdensome task. We do have control over ourselves, whether or not we acknowledge our feelings, our attitudes about ourselves, and all of our behaviors. But there are many other things that we don't have control over, such as other people's feelings, attitudes, and behaviors. We don't know what will happen tomorrow, and we can't change what happened yesterday. It's not your fault that you were abused or that you may have some problems because you were abused. But it is within your power to heal from the negative affects of your experiences. This is your task today.

Jerry told me about how he came to understand how his higher power allowed him to surrender control:

Once I came to believe in a greater power, I knew there was someone watching over me and He had a plan that I was not aware of. That meant that I didn't have to control everything so much. I was able to kick back and let things happen. I knew He was taking care of some things and sooner or later it would become evident to me what I needed to do.

Relinquishing control doesn't mean that you give up altogether. It means that you have come to terms with the fact that there are some things you cannot control. The serenity prayer that is recited at Alcoholics Anonymous meetings reminds us of this fact: "God grant me the serenity to accept the things I cannot change, the courage to change the things I can, and the wisdom to know the difference."

Over time, Jerry came to realize that giving up control didn't mean giving up responsibility:

> After a while I began to realize that I couldn't leave everything up to my higher power. I had to do my part. There were things within my control, such as my problems with my temper, that I had to attend to and it was up to me deal with those things. The rest I would have to leave up to Him.

Mark relinquished control by first realizing that he needed help during his time of crisis. He couldn't do it alone. Turning to a higher power helped him feel a greater sense of peace. He also realized that he would need professional help to deal with his problems resulting from the abuse. He found a therapist who helped him work through his childhood abuse. By writing down and interpreting his dreams with his therapist, he learned about the wisdom of his unconscious, a part of him that he knew very little about. He got in touch with powerful feelings, began to examine his attitudes, and understand how these would manifest in behaviors. He learned that through his dreams he could develop a better understanding of himself, and in doing so would make better choices in his life. By facing his relationship with his higher power he ultimately felt more connected to himself.

Feeling Connected to the Collective

Spirituality also helps people feel a closer connection to the greater humankind. It does this because believing in a higher power transcends money, possessions, politics, borders, race, and many other material objects and principles that are often used to separate or differentiate people. Because spirituality is something that happens within you, no one can take it away from you. It is something that you take with you everywhere you go. And because it knows no bounds it can be something that connects you to all people no matter how much our personal thoughts, prejudices, or judgments try to interfere.

Sam describes how his spirituality helps him feel connected to other people:

> When I communicate with my higher power I have this feeling that I am somehow more connected to all things and people—future, present, and past. I feel as though I am part of a greater plan. It doesn't make me feel insignificant; on the contrary, I feel I am an important part of the play.

Developing your spirituality is going beyond yourself. It is viewing life from a broader perspective that can bring you a sense of peace and tranquility by letting go. When you let go of trying to control everything that happens to you and the people around you, you are likely to feel a release, a freedom to be yourself without the burdensome responsibility that goes along with needing to control.

However you understand God, spirituality, or a higher power, it is important to think about how it can help you during your healing process. Certainly during the moments when you are most desperate for help, when you feel the greatest pain, when you are most lost, you can rely on that part of yourself that you may ordinarily ignore. However, if you learn to use your spirituality on a daily basis you may discover that it can help you during the happy moments as well as the painful times.

Ask yourself the following questions to examine the role your spirituality can play in your healing process:

How Can You Use Your Spirituality During Your Healing Journey?

- What does spirituality mean to you?

- What role does spirituality play in your life?

- How can you use your spirituality in your healing journey (i.e., during times of crisis or intense emotional upheaval or to relinquish control, ask for help, or feel a closer connection to the collective)?

Healing Through Peer Support Groups

In addition to individual counseling, another way to heal is through peer support groups consisting of other adult survivors of childhood abuse. There are now such support groups across the country. Giving and receiving support from men who are struggling with similar issues can facilitate your healing process and at the same time lessen the sense of isolation and alienation you may be feeling. Support groups can also help you learn new skills and ways of dealing with personal and relationship problems.

The groups I have led have become a laboratory for men learning to experiment with new behaviors and attitudes. Frequently men develop friendships with other men in the group. These friendships share not only a certain history but also new values they are learning within the group. Few men can talk easily about their true inner feelings with other men. However, when men develop friendships outside of their support group they already have the experience of talking about their feelings with each other. This makes having such conversations outside of the group much easier. Another advantage of support groups is having a number of men to count on for support in case of a crisis, rather than on a therapist. Having the choice of five or six people to call who know you and your issues during a time of need can greatly alleviate the anxiety of feeling alone in your recovery. Finally, the support group for healing from childhood abuse can put you in touch with people who are further along on the road to recovery. These contacts can help you learn from the mistakes of others and learn about the many ways people approach their healing. What is most important here is recognizing that you cannot solve this problem alone. This is not meant to be an admission of weakness or sickness but a realization that whatever work you can do on your own will be greatly facilitated by the support of others. It is like the story of the man who called on the rabbi, asking the difference between heaven and hell. The rabbi took the man into a room that had a large table. Sitting around this table were people who looked terrible. They were hungry, miserable, depressed—just awful. In the middle of the table was a large bowl of soup. Each person had a long spoon that was long enough to reach the bowl of soup but too long to put the soup in his mouth. The rabbi said, "This is hell." Then he took the man into another room, and there too was a large table with a bowl of soup in the middle. The people here also had long soup spoons in their hands that barely reached the soup but were too long to put the soup in their mouths. However, the people sitting around this table looked nourished, happy, and content. The rabbi said, "This is heaven." The man said, "Rabbi, how is it that these people look so good, but like the others are unable to get the soup in their mouths?" The rabbi replied, "Because these individuals have learned to feed each other."

We must learn how to get fed by and feed others. Isolation only exacerbates whatever problems exist as a result of childhood abuse. Counseling, whether it is individual, group, couple, or family, will decrease isolation and increase your options.

One Day at a Time

Some men who come into my office want a guarantee that I can help them heal from the abuse immediately. You may want a quick fix that will enable you to change your behaviors and problems for the rest of your life. Or you may be feeling a pressure that if you act out again your family will fall apart or you will go to jail. You may feel as though you are walking on eggshells. How can you stop a lifelong pattern immediately? By taking one day at a time. This is all you can do. Every day you have to wake up and do the best you can do to heal. You need a plan just for that day. You may decide when you wake up that you want to focus on a specific issue relating to recovery. For example:

- Today I am going to work on not stuffing my anger. Today I am going to think about my old baggage and write about my abuse in my journal.

- Today I am going to pray for guidance from my higher power and seek help through counseling.

These commitments are quite a lot to accomplish in one day, but making a concerted effort to change your behavior takes work! Don't forget, you will have an inner tendency to forget about your problems when they are not staring you in the face. That is why recovering from childhood abuse takes a daily plan of action. Make a plan for today. What can you do in the next twenty-four hours to begin to heal from childhood abuse?

WOUNDED
HEROES

The late Joseph Campbell, author of numerous books on philosophy and mythology, wrote an entire book about heroes and heroism entitled *The Hero with a Thousand Faces*. In it he discusses the concept of the hero's journey as seen by differing cultures and as reflected in art and literature. He found a universal theme surrounding heroism. It was quite consistent between different societies, and the same themes were repeated throughout the history of those cultures. This book so inspired director George Lucas that he created a series of contemporary films about the hero's journey, entitled *Star Wars*.

When I first read about the hero's journey I immediately related it to the healing process from childhood abuse. I realized that each of us who embarks on a dangerous endeavor is a hero. It takes a great deal of courage to face your inner wounds. None of us likes to look at our weaknesses or vulnerabilities. But only by doing so can you come to terms with your abuse and the personal problems that resulted. Understanding the phases of the hero's journey as outlined by Campbell will help you see how the hero's journey relates to your own healing process.

The classic hero's journey has four stages: the calling, the leaving, the courageous act, and the return. Let's look more closely at what characterizes each stage.

The Calling

Every hero's journey begins with a message sent to the potential hero, either from within or from elsewhere. The hero may experience the internal message as uneasiness, discomfort, or a feeling that something is just not right. The message may also come from someone else, either in verbal or written form. For example, your partner or a friend may tell you that you need to solve your personal problems. Many men have embarked on their inner journey because the court mandated counseling.

Think about how you came to recognize your own calling. Perhaps you felt inside that something was not right, unresolved, or uncomfortable. It may have been your own inner need to heal that brought you this far, or your calling may have come from someone else. You may have read a book or a newspaper article or watched a television program or movie that motivated you to embark on a healing journey. Both the internal and external messages are there, but if the hero doesn't respond, the messages get more extreme until they fall on your head like a hundred-pound weight. Divorce, separation, and arrests for violence or drug abuse are just a few of these overt messages that we get.

At some point the hero decides whether or not to respond. If he doesn't, the messages simply become more demonstrative. If he does choose to acknowledge the calling, he is faced with the next task in his journey, the leaving.

Once the hero heeds the call he must depart from a safe place and venture into uncharted territory. Breaking the denial that has kept you safe all these years and talking about long-ignored feelings, thoughts, and memories may be the first step on your journey.

The Leaving

Embarking on your healing journey can be frightening and unnerving. You are out of your daily routine, which removes your sense of predictability and security. The healing process can be like a roller coaster; sometimes you will feel frightened, angry, and depressed, and other times you will feel energized, excited, and hopeful. Most important, the leaving means you must come face to face with unfamiliar parts of yourself, both positive and negative.

What makes this frightening part of the journey a little easier is the presence of a spirit guide or mentor who will assist your transition into the unknown. In the movie *Star Wars*, Ben Kenobi helped Luke Skywalker across the threshold from earth to space and taught him the importance of getting in touch with his own inner force. Your spirit guide may take the form of a therapist, another man who is already on his healing journey, an AA sponsor, a close friend, or a lover. Your guide can be just about anyone you respect and trust and who has taken a similar journey. Ultimately this guide will help you prepare for the most challenging part of your journey, the courageous act.

At some point in his journey the hero is faced with a challenge of enormous proportions. He may have to do battle with a frightening creature or another person. He may have to reclaim a treasure that was taken away or save the life of another person. Usually the hero has to use not only his physical strength but other resources, such as feeling, intelligence, intuition, or sensitivity. The hero has to put aside his ego, become humble, and do what is necessary to complete the task.

The Courageous Act

You will find many challenges in healing from childhood abuse. Perhaps you will have to do battle with your inner abuser or reclaim your lost inner child or rescue your own inner feminine/feeling side. You will have to do battle with your inner abuser's tendency to blame you for the abuse. Combating low self-esteem is another challenge of the healing process. Learning to get in touch with your feelings may be the greatest challenge of all. You will face other inner challenges, such as acknowledging your weaknesses, admitting that you can't do it alone, being willing to make and learn from your mistakes, and learning to ask for help. This will require courage and persistence, but when you return you will have changed in a fundamental way.

The Return

When the hero returns from his journey there is something different about him. The courageous act has brought about an inner change that others notice immediately. Your partner, friends, or coworkers may tell you that you seem different. You may even notice the difference yourself, feel more centered, at peace with yourself, or happier with life. You may not feel noticeably different from the way you felt last week, but you may feel radically different than you did six months or a year ago.

An important part of the hero's return is talking about what he has learned on his way. This doesn't mean bragging about his heroism but spreading an important message that captures the essence of the journey. For you this may involve encouraging other men to embark on a similar healing journey. It may also simply be encouraging others to talk about their feelings rather than hide them. You may find that your message will go to your children in that you choose to raise them differently from the way you were raised. It may be helping a friend in crisis or supporting your partner in a different way than you have in the past. Some men have written about their experiences in the hope that other men could find courage in hearing another man's story.

Heroes usually don't go on only one journey; adventure is a way of life for them. There is a continual leaving and returning, coming and going, facing new challenges and reaching new heights of awareness and change. Your healing journey will consist of a similar process of leaving a safe and comfortable place, facing and meeting a challenge, and returning with a new attitude or other change. After a while you will venture out again to face new hurdles and overcome new barriers to finding peace of mind. But with each journey you will develop new skills to make the next one easier.

Facing the intense pain of childhood abuse takes courage of heroic proportions. You are a hero for answering the call no matter in what form it came. You are a hero for asking for help and taking deliberate steps in healing your wounds. You are a hero for facing your inner demons and reclaiming your lost self. You are a hero for coming back a changed person and passing on your knowledge to others. You are a hero for continuing to struggle with your wounds and make peace with yourself and others. Through your healing journey you will discover your own heroism and learn to appreciate the heroism in others.

Leaving and Returning

How to Start a
Self-help
Wounded-Men's
Group

The issue of wounded men is only recently being recognized by our society, so many communities lack services in the form of self-help groups. The problem is compounded by the fact that many men have difficulty acknowledging their need for help and support. If this is the case in your community, you may want to start your own group. It may take some work, but with the help of others it is possible. Find someone who will help you with the planning and logistics. There are likely to be headaches in the process, and having someone to share frustrations will be a blessing. In addition, the more people who plan the group the more good ideas will surface in the process.

Before you reach out to other men you need to make sure you

have a time and place available to hold your meetings. Churches, banks, community centers, and civic centers all have meetings rooms available to nonprofit community groups. It is also not unusual for a counseling agency to donate space for a self-help group. Call around, and don't be afraid to be up front with the person at the other end of the line. Tell them you are looking for donated space for a self-help recovery group for men who were abused as children. You may want to talk with other self-help groups in your community, such as Alcoholics Anonymous or Parents United. These groups may be valuable resources to help you learn what steps you need to take to get your group off the ground. You do not need to reinvent the wheel.

Getting the Word Out

The first step is to make the group's presence known in the community. You may do this through, fliers, public speaking, advertising, and word of mouth. Speaking to local organizations such as Rotary or Chamber of Commerce, churches, schools, mental-health agencies, shelters for battered women, child-abuse programs, and employee-assistance programs will help to raise the community's consciousness about this problem. When radio and television find out about your self-help group, they may want to interview some of your members. The media are an excellent way to reach many potential members, at no cost! Public-service announcements on the radio and television are other ways to reach out to men in your community.

Setting the Rules

In order for any group to run smoothly it is necessary that the members agree to rules and are clear about expectations. You may want to add the following group rules, which are useful in any self-help group:

- Do not interrupt when people are talking.

- Do not talk with other group members when someone is talking.

- Try not to give advice unless asked for—talk about your feelings.

- Start on time, end on time.

- Confidentiality: What is said here, stays here.

- No touching without permission from others.

- No alcohol or drugs 24 hours before group.

- No eating or drinking during sessions.

- Keep to the structure of the group.

- Decide on whether or not a facilitator is needed.

- Honesty, Open-mindedness, Willingness.

You may want to elect officers, such as treasurer (responsible for collecting money, bank deposits, and so on), facilitator (leads group for that session or series), administrator (plans meetings, secures meeting space, and so on), and educator (responsible for community outreach). You may eventually want to develop a list of crisis lines and resources in the community in case group members experience a crisis between sessions. Members could also exchange personal phone numbers as a way of maintaining support between sessions and encouraging communication. A newcomer to Alcoholics Anonymous is encouraged to find a sponsor, a more experienced member who is familiar with the program and the recovery process, who will help him learn how to make use of the program and offer support during times of crisis. You may decide to develop a similar concept in your group. Talk about it with the group.

The Group Check-in

Once a group has six or eight members, even if you meet for one and a half or two hours, not every man will have the opportunity to talk about his particular issues. This is okay. Often we can learn about ourselves by simply listening to others. A group check-in can partly address this issue by giving every man the opportunity to touch base briefly with the rest of the group about his progress in his healing journey. At the beginning of each group, each member can disclose the highlights of his week with regard to healing. The group may decide to have an unstructured check-in, asking, "How was your week?" or it may be in the form of specific questions.

- What is your name?

- What type of abuse did you experience as a child?

- What is the issue, with regard to healing, that you are concerned about?

Using This Book in Your Groups

Wounded Boys, Heroic Men can be utilized in counselor-led groups or peer-led self-help groups to structure the group sessions. For example, group members can read the book at home and bring particular issues or exercises of concern to them to each session. Or specific chapters could be assigned for each session. Below is a list of the exercises in this book by chapter as well as additional suggestions for group discussions. Don't be afraid to use your creativity. If a discussion goes in a particularly interesting direction that is not mentioned here, go for it.

Chapter 1: Wounded Men, Wounded Boys

During your first meeting you will need to discuss the group rules and expectations. You can also decide on a check-in process at this session. Once the business is taken care of, group members need to introduce themselves to one another. Each man may want to talk about what brought him to the group at this point in his life. For example, was there a crisis or simply a need to deal with old problems stemming from abuse? Perhaps a newcomer may be there to find out if he was abused or, if he was, how the abuse has caused problems in his life.

Getting to know each other by talking about personal problems and experiences can be difficult at first. Chances are that you will all have come from different backgrounds and experiences, but you are likely to have many things in common. Focus on the similarities, not just the differences. In this way members can form a bond that makes support and learning from each other possible.

Additional Exercises

• What has brought you to this group?

• What would you like to get out of the experience?

Chapter 2: Preparation for Your Journey

As you start facing your inner wounds, it will be helpful for you to discuss your thoughts and feelings along the way, especially when things get uncomfortable. This should be a given in all sessions. In this early meeting, however, it may be useful to predict how you may react and what you will do when it happens. You will find that some men are more prone to depression or withdrawal, and others are more prone to anger. Brainstorming ways of preventing slipping back into denial or feeling overwhelmed can be helpful in the long run.

Additional Exercises

• What reactions have you had so far in your healing journey?

• Which techniques described in the chapter can you imagine using to deal with these reactions?

Chapter 3: The Abuse and the Wounds

Talking about childhood experiences of abuse and their effects can be very threatening, but it can also be relieving to know that you are not the only person who has had a particular experience or problem. Each man can begin this group by discussing the types of abuse he experienced as a child and how he believes the abused affected him today.

Although many men intuitively know that what they experienced was abuse, others may not be so certain. It is important to respect each group member's thoughts and feelings about this issue. For example, if another man says that he is not sure if his father touching him on his penis was abuse it may be valuable for him to hear what you think—but you do not need to convince him of your point of view. In fact, he may get turned off or feel abused if group members are trying to change his mind or make him think about his experience in a particular way. It is important to respect someone's thoughts and feelings, even if the person refuses to see the writing on the wall. Every man has his own timing for coming to terms with his abuse.

Additional Exercises

- What type of abuse have you experienced?

- What did you do to cope with the abuse?

- How did you feel then?

- How do you feel now?

Chapter 4: Breaking Denial: "I Was an Abused Child."

In this chapter there are specific exercises that may provide a structure for discussion and for breaking denial. For example, group members could discuss rationalizations they have used to deny their experiences. Those who are ready can say to each man in the group, "I was abused." Likewise, if you are comfortable doing so, talking about specifics of the abuse can help to relieve the tension of keeping secrets. It is important for group members to talk about their feelings throughout the process, both in talking about their problems as well as giving feedback to other group members.

Exercises

- How do you rationalize your abusive experiences?

- Were you abused?

- Can you say the words?

- What specifics come to mind?

- How does it feel to read about your abuse?

- How has the abuse affected you today?

- Who can you tell?

Additional Exercises

- What specific changes would you like to make in this group?

- How could the other group members help in this process?

Chapter 5: Healing Through Feelings

You could discuss the material in this chapter eight hours a day for weeks and it still wouldn't be enough. However, several sessions devoted exclusively to the topic of healing through feelings would be a valuable experience for all men. The exercise for feeling-avoidance patterns is an excellent way to begin the discussion of how men deal with their feelings. Because anger is such a common reaction to childhood abuse, focusing on that emotion is an important step in the healing process.

Each group member could identify his physical and behavioral cues to anger. How do you deal with these feelings? Are you a stuffer, escalater, or director? Give personal examples of each type. Men frequently talk about their trouble differentiating today's anger and yesterday's anger from old baggage. Each man may want to talk about experiences he has had with each type and how he expressed himself. It is equally crucial to identify and communicate other feelings, such as sadness, fear, and hurt. You can use the feelings journal to record feelings that occur between sessions, and bring it to each group session to help you focus on your healing issues and give you experience in identifying and communicating all feelings.

Exercises

- How do you avoid your feelings?

- How did your family express anger?

Additional Exercises

- How do you communicate anger?

- How do you communicate other feelings?

- What are the physical and behavioral signs of your anger?

- How can you utilize the feelings journal? Can you give an example of some feelings you experienced this week?

- How do you stuff, escalate, and direct your feelings? Give examples for two or three different feelings (sadness, fear, hurt, joy, and so on).

- Give an example of how you communicate today's anger.

- Give an example of how you communicated yesterday's anger.

- Give an example of how you brought old baggage into your communication.

You can complete and discuss any of the exercises in the context of a group. The description of and dialogue with the inner abuser could be a profound experience for each man in the group. Place an empty chair in the middle of the circle. Each man can take his own turn placing his inner abuser in that chair and having dialogue with him or her. First, describe for the group members the inner abuser, then tell him or her your feelings and thoughts about him and how he affects you.

Chapter 6: Healing Through Attitudes

- What are your negative self-talk messages?

Exercises

- Who is your inner abuser?

- Can you transform negative to positive self-talk?

- Can you tell yourself, I was not responsible for the abuse?

- Can you take risks?

- How can you learn to trust?

Additional Exercises

- How have your experiences with abuse affected your attitude toward men? Women?

When a man brings problems relating to violence and chemical abuse to the group, it is important to deal directly with those issues so that healing can progress. For example, if a man has a chemical addiction, healing will not occur unless he addresses that problem because the addiction will prevent him from dealing with the

Chapter 7: Healing Through Behaviors

feelings, attitudes, and behaviors related to the abuse. Likewise, if violence is occurring in a man's life, he must first make sure that he and others are safe so that he can address the underlying issues that bring about the violent behaviors. These issues should be discussed in the group; but because of the potential harm chemical addictions and violence present to you and others, additional action may need to be taken to address those particular problems. Group discussions can focus on the role of addictions in your life, abusive patterns toward others, and brainstorming ways to break destructive patterns of coping with problems. Referrals to Alcoholics Anonymous, Narcotics Anonymous, and anger-management programs can be made to individuals experiencing chemical abuse and/or violence. In addition, there are numerous books a man can read that help to address these issues as well (see Suggested Reading).

Process addictions, though serious, do not necessarily present the danger to self or others that chemical addictions and violence do. There may also be specialty groups in your community that address such problems as sexual addictions, relationship addictions, and so on. This is not to say that these issues shouldn't be discussed in the group but that additional referrals may need to be made to prevent behavior problems from getting worse.

Exercises

- Can you take responsibility for your violence?

- What role do chemicals play in your life?

- What role do process addictions play in your life?

Additional Exercises

- Is violence a problem in your life? If yes, how so?

- How can the time-out help you deal better with your anger?

- What are ways you can talk yourself down?

Although most men avoid discussing sexual concerns, it is an area that has special relevance for men who were abused as children, especially men who were sexually abused. Having a group that focuses on sexual fears, concerns, and problems will help to break a typical pattern that men use to avoid being real with each other. More often, you probably joke about sex, make innuendos, and suggest that it is not a problem for you or your partner. It is not uncommon for men to experience difficulties in the sexual arena relating to sexual desire, functioning, attitudes, and feelings.

Chapter 8: Healing Through Sexuality

- How can you communicate your sexual needs?

Exercises

- Which of the sexual myths described do you believe?

Additional Exercises

- Do you have negative feelings about sex?

- How did the abuse affect your sexual feeling, attitudes, or behaviors?

- Do you experience any fears that you might abuse others?

Though not all men are ready actually to speak with their abuser early in the healing process, it is important for all men at least to vent their feelings about the abuser. As in the exercise with the inner abuser, placing the abuser in a chair and entering into a dialogue with him or her can be a cathartic experience. This can be a safe opportunity to explore your feelings about this person and get them off your chest. With the support of group peers you can express pent-up feelings and relieve some of the pressure. Should you have ongoing contact with the abuser or decide to confront that person with your feelings, an exercise like this will better prepare you for that interaction. Role-play the abuser's minimization and denial with other members. Talk about options for the man who doesn't have contact with his abuser. Discuss what has to happen for forgiveness to occur, and if you can find peace without forgiveness.

Chapter 9: Making Peace with Your Abuser

Additional Exercises

- Why do you want to confront your abuser?

- Preparing for your initial contact:
  - What thoughts I want to tell him?

  - What feelings I want to tell him?

  - What I want from him?
- What if he/she minimizes the abuse?

- What if he/she denies the abuse?

- What if he/she is unavailable?

- Is forgiveness possible?

Chapter 10: Making Peace with Yourself

Spirituality can be an important part of your healing process for the reasons described in the chapter. You may decide to have an open-ended discussion about this topic or structure the conversation with specific questions. What does spirituality mean to you? How do you think it can help you in your healing journey? The transformation process involves achieving an inner balance. What parts of yourself would you like to see more in balance? How can you go about making that happen? Change occurs by taking little steps one day at a time. What plan of action can you take right now to reach your goals?

Exercises

- What does spirituality mean to you?

- What role does spirituality play in your life?

- How can you use your spirituality during your healing process (that is, during times of crisis or intense emotional upheaval, to relinquish control, to ask for help, or to feel a closer connection to others)?

Additional Exercises

- What inner qualities do you have that are in need of more balance?

- How can you take one day at a time?

Appendix II

SUGGESTED READINGS

This is not an exhaustive review of the literature on each subject, rather a list of books that I have personally reviewed and found helpful in addressing the issue of male victimization. I may have inadvertently left out other excellent books in each subject area. My apology to other authors.

Evan, P. (1996). *Childhood Hurts*. New York: Bantam.

Farmer, Steven (1989). *Adult Children of Abusive Parents: A Healing Program for Those Who Have Been Physically, Sexually, or Psychologically Abused*. Los Angeles: Lowell House.

Gannon, Patrick J. (1989). *Soul Survivors: A New Beginning for Adults Abused as Children*. New York: Prentice Hall.

Gil, Eliana (1983). *Outgrowing the Pain: A Book for and About Adults Abused as Children*. San Francisco: Launch Press.

Kempe, C. H. and Hefler, R. E. (1980). *The Battered Child*. Chicago: University of Chicago Press.

Krupinski, Eve and Weikel, Dana (N.D.). *Death from Child Abuse: And No One Heard*. Gulf Breeze, FL: Currier/Davis Publishing.

Miller, Alice (1984). *For Your Own Good: Hidden Cruelty in Childrearing and the Roots of Violence*. New York: Farrar, Straus and Giroux.

Miller, Alice (1986). *Thou Shalt Not Be Aware: Society's Betrayal of the Child*. New York: American Library.

Mones, Paul (1991). *When a Child Kills: Abused Children Who Kill Their Parents*. New York: Pocket Books.

Physical Abuse

Morris, Gregory (1985). *The Kids Next Door: Sons and Daughters Who Kill Their Parents*. New York: Morrow.

Straus, Murray A. and Donnelly, Denise (1994). *A Beating the Devil Out of Them: Corporal Punishment in American Families*. New York: Toronto: Lexington Books.

Sexual Abuse   Allen, Craig (1991). *Women and Men Who Sexually Abuse Children: A Comparative Analysis*. Brandon, VT: Safer Society Press.

Bain, Ouaine and Sanders, Maureen (1990). *Out in the Open: A Guide for Young People Who Have Been Sexually Abused*. London: Virago Upstarts.

Berkshire County Rape Crisis Center (1988). *It Happens to Boys Too*. Pittsfield, MA: Berkshire County Rape Crisis Center.

Butler, Sandra (1978; updated 1985). *Conspiracy of Silence: The Trauma of Incest*. Volcano: Volcano Press.

Davis, Laura (1990). *The Courage to Heal Workbook: For Men and Women Survivors of Sexual Abuse*. New York: Harper & Row.

Dimock, Peter and Euan Bear (1988). *Adults Molested as Children: A Survivor's Manual for Women and Men*. Orwell, VT: Safer Society Press.

Estrada, H. (1994). *Recovery for Male Victims of Child Sexual Abuse*. Santa Fe: Red Rabbit Press.

Grubman-Black, Stephen (1990). *Broken Boys/Mending Men: Recovery From Childhood Sexual Abuse*. New York: Ivy Books.

Herman, Judith L. (1992). *Trauma and Recovery*. New York: Basic Books.

Hunter, Mic (1990). *Abused Boys: The Neglected Victims of Sexual Abuse*. New York: Fawcett Columbine.

Incest Survivors Anonymous. *I.S.A. Tales to Friends, Survivors, and Professionals*. Long Beach, CA: ISA World Services.

Incest Survivors Anonymous. *The Twelve Steps of Sexual Abuse Anonymous*. Long Beach, CA: ISA World Services.

Incest Survivors Anonymous. *Welcome to the Newcomer*. Long Beach, CA: ISA World Services.

Kempe, R. and Kempe, C. H. (1984). *The Common Secret: Sexual Abuse of Children and Adolescents*. New York: W. H. Freeman.

Kunzman, Kristin (1990). *The Healing Way: Adult Recovery from Childhood Sexual Abuse.* San Francisco: Harper and Row.

Lee, Sharice A. (1995). *The Survivor's Guide.* Thousand Oaks, CA: Sage Publications, Inc.

Lew, Mike (1990). *Victims No Longer: Men Recovering From Incest.* New York: Harper and Row.

Maltz, Wendy and Holman, Beverly (1987). *Incest and Sexuality: A Guide to Understanding and Healing.* Lexington, MA: Lexington.

Masson, Jeffrey Moussaieff (1985). *The Assault on Truth: Freuds Suppression of the Seduction Theory.* New York: Penguin Books.

Mather, Cynthia L. and Debye, Kristina E. (1994). *How Long Does It Hurt?: A Guide to Recovering From Incest and Sexual Abuse for Teenagers, Their Friends and Their Families.* San Francisco: Jossey-Bass, ©1994. HV 6570.7 .M37.

Mendel, Matthew Parynik. (1995). *The Male Survivor: The Impact of Sexual Abuse.* Thousand Oaks, CA: Sage Publications, Inc.

Pryor, Douglas W. (1996). *Unspeakable Acts: Why Men Sexually Abuse Children.* New York: New York University Press.

Rowley, Thelma (1986). *Touches and Feelings.* Queenlands (Australia) Center for the Prevention of Child Abuse.

Rush, Florence (1980). *The Best Kept Secret: Sexual Abuse of Children.* Englewood Cliffs, NJ: Prentice-Hall.

Sanders, Timothy (1991). *Male Survivors: Twelve-step Recovery Program for Survivors of Childhood Sexual Abuse.* Freedom, CA: Crossing Press.

Psychological Abuse

Miller, Alice (1991). *Breaking Down the Wall of Silence: The Liberating Experience of Facing the Painful Truth.* New York: Dutton.

Miller, Alice (1990). *The Untouched Key: Tracing Childhood Trauma in Creativity and Destructiveness.* New York: Anchor.

Miller, Alice (1990). *Banished Knowledge: Facing Childhood Injuries.* New York: Anchor Books

Miller, Alice (1981). *The Drama of the Gifted Child: How Narcissistic Parents Form and Deform the Emotional Lives of Their Talented Children.* New York: Basic Books.

Partner Abuse   Davis, Diane (1984). *Something Is Wrong in My House.* Seattle: Parenting Press.

Dutton, Don (1995). *The Batterer.* New York: Harper Collins.

Gelles, Richard and Straus, Murray (1988). *Intimate Violence: The Definitive Study of the Causes and Consequences of Abuse in the American Family.* New York: Simon and Schuster.

Gondolf, Edward and Russell, David (1987). *Man to Man: A Guide for Men in Abusive Relationships.* Brandenton, FL: Human Services Institute, Inc.

Island, D. and Letellier, P. (1991). *Men Who Beat Men Who Love Them: Battered Gay Men and Domestic Violence.* New York: Harrington Park.

McKay, Matthew, McKay, Judith, and Rogers, Peter (1989). *When Anger Hurts: Quieting the Storm Within.* Oakland, CA: New Harbinger Publications.

Paymar, M. (1993). *Violent No More: Helping Men End Domestic Violence.* Alameda, CA: Hunter House.

Sonkin, Daniel and Durphy, Michael (1989 rev.) *Learning to Live Without Violence: A Handbook for Men.* Volcano, CA: Volcano Press.

Appendix III

A SELECTION OF
NATIONAL RESOURCES

This is not an exhaustive list of all the national resouces on abuse, but rather a list of organizations that may be helpful in finding local self-help and counseling resources. I may have inadvertently left out other excellent organizations who are committed to addressing the problem of violence in the family. Should you want your organization to be considered for future editions, please feel free to contact me in care of Adams Media Corporation.

Al-Anon Family Groups, Inc. (or look up in your local white pages)
Box 182, Madison Square Station
New York, N.Y. 10159

Alcoholics Anonymous (or look up in your local white pages)
World Headquarters
Box 459, Grand Central Station
New York, N.Y. 10163

C. Henry Kempe National Center for the Prevention and Treatment of Child Abuse and Neglect.
1205 Oneida Street
Denver, Colorado 80220
303-321-3963

Center for Child Protection and Family Support
People of Color Leadership Institute (POCLI)
714 G. Street, SE
Washington, DC 20003
202-544-3144

Family Violence & Sexual Assault Institute
1310 Clinic Drive
Tyler, TX 75701
903-595-6600

Incest Survivors Anonymous
P.O. Box 5613
Long Beach, CA 90805-0613
213-428-5599

Legal Council for the Elderly
Legal Hotline: 800-424-3410

Narcotic's Anonymous (or look up in your local white pages)
World Service Office
P.O. Box 9999
Van Nuys, CA 91409

National Center on Elder Abuse
810 First St., NE, Suite 500
Washington, DC 20002-4267
202-682-2470

National Clearinghouse for Alcohol
and Drug Information (NCADI)
11426 Rockville Pike, Suite 200
Rockville, MD 20852
800-729-6686
301-468-2600

National Clearinghouse on Child
Abuse and Neglect
P.O. Box 1182
Washington, DC 20013
703-385-7565

National Coalition Against Domestic
Violence
P.O. Box 34103
Washington, D.C. 20043-4103
703-765-0339
P.O. Box 18749
Denver, CO 80218-0749
303-839-1852

National Committee for Prevention
of Child Abuse
332 South Michigan Ave, Suite 1600
Chicago, Illinois 60604-4357
312-663-3520

National Council to Prevent Child
Abuse and Family Violence
1155 Connecticut Ave NW, Suite 400
Washington, DC 20036
202-429-6695

National Domestic Violence/
Abuse Hotline
800-799-SAFE
800-799-7233
800-787-3224 TDD

National Gay and Lesbian Domestic
Violence Victim's Network
3506 S. Ouray Circle
Aurora, CO 80013
303-266-3477

National Self-Help Clearing House
CUNY-New York
25 West 43rd Street, #620
New York, NY 10036
212-345-8525
212-642-2944

Parents Anonymous (Child abuse)
6733 S. Sepulveda Boulevard
Los Angeles, CA 90045
213-419-9732

Parents United (Child sexual abuse)
Adults Molested as Children United
P.O. Box 952
San Jose, CA 95108
408-280-5055

P.L.E.A. (Prevention, Leadership,
Education, and Assistance) (Sexual,
physical, emotional abuse, and neglect)
Hank Astrada, Founder and Director
P.O. Box 291182
Los Angeles, CA 90029
213-254-9962

V.O.I.C.E.S. (Victims of Incest Can
Emerge Survivors)
P.O. Box 148309
Chicago, Ill. 60614
312-327-1500

Local Counseling Resources
Look up in the Yellow Pages*:

Alcoholism Information & Treatment
Centers
Battered Persons' Aid
Child Abuse & Neglect
Drug Abuse & Addiction Information
and Treatment Centers
Marriage, Family, and Child Counselors
Physicians - Psychiatry
Psychologists
Social Service Organizations
Social Workers

*Courtesy of the Pacific Bell Smart Yellow Pages

Appendix IV

A SELECTION OF INTERNET RESOURCES

A Guide to Psychotherapy on the World Wide Web
  http://www.shef.ac.uk/uni/projects/gpp/index.htm/
America Online Online Psych
  Keyword: psychology
Abuse Survivors' Resources
  http://www.tezcat.com/~tina/psych.shtml
The Association of Recovering Abuse Survivors and Offenders
  http://www.areason.org/
Beverly Greene's Child Abuse and Rape Survivors' Resources
  http://www.geocities.com/WestHollywood/1769/survivor.html
The Big Page of Information for Survivors
  http://www.fiber.net/users/jeffglo/nik.htm
Domestic Violence and Child Abuse Resources
  http://members.aol.com/dsonkin/index.html
Domestic Violence Hotline Resource
  http://www.feminist.org/911/crisis.html
Emotional Trauma Info Pages - David Baldwin
  http://gladstone.uoregon.edu/~dvb/trauma.htm
For Loved Ones of Sexual Assault/Abuse Survivors
  http://www.odos.uiuc.edu/Counseling_Center/friends.htm
Jim Hopper Child Abuse Resources
  http://www.jimhopper.com/
M.A.L.E. - Men Assisting Leading & Educating
  http://www.malesurvivor.org/
Men and Domestic Violence Index
  http://www.vix.com/pub/men/domestic-index.html

Mental Health Net Self-Help Abuse Resources
http://www.cmhcsys.com/guide/abuse.htm

National Crisis Prevention Institute
http://www.execpc.com/~cpi/index.html

Not Victims!
http://www.unc.edu/~juliette/notvictims.html

On the Road to Healing
http://www.geocities.com/HotSprings/2891/

Parents and Loved Ones of Sexual Abuse and Rape Victims
http://www.geocities.com/HotSprings/2656/

Partners Against Violence
http://www.usdoj.gov/pavnet.html

Psychological Self-Help
http://www.cmhc.com/psyhelp/

Ritual Abuse and Healing Home Page
http://www.xroads.com/rahome/

Safeguarding Our Children - United Mothers
http://www.tracy.org/soc-um/

The Safer Society Foundation, Inc.
http://www.merrymac.com/safer/safesoc.html

SafetyNet
http://www.cybergrrl.com/dv.html

Sanctuary
http://www.artsci.wustl.edu/~chack/sanct/sanctuary.html

Surviving Child Sexual Abuse
http://www.odos.uiuc.edu/Counseling_Center/sexab.htm

The Survivor's Page
http://cam043212.student.utwente.nl

Survivors and Victims Empowered (SAVE)
http://www.goshen.net/SAVE/

The Survivors' Voice
http://www.billboards.com/billboards/tsv/

What Men Can do to End Violence Against Women
http://www.cs.utk.edu/~bartley/other/realMen.html

The Wounded Healer Home Page
http://idealist.com/wounded_healer/

Appendix V

THE HERO'S JOURNEY

The late Joseph Campbell's description of the hero's journey is much like healing from childhood abuse. Each of us who embarks on a dangerous endeavor is a hero. It takes a great deal of courage to face your inner wounds. By facing your inner demons, and coming to terms with your vulnerabilities you re-emerge a changed person—transformed by the process.

The Calling

The hero's journey begins with a calling; a message sent to him from far away. He may experience the message as an inner uneasiness, discomfort, or a feeling that something is just not right. The message may also come from outside the hero in the form of someone else telling him he needs to change.

The Leaving

Now the hero must depart from a safe place and venture into uncharted territory. This begins with breaking the denial that has kept you safe all these years and talking about long-ignored feelings, thoughts and memories.

Embarking on your healing journey can be frightening and unnerving. You are out of your daily routine which removes your sense of predictability and security. Most important, the leaving means you must come face to face with different parts of yourself, both positive and negative.

The Spirit Guide

Every hero has the assistance of a spirit guide or mentor; someone who has also taken the journey and who will assist you in your process. Your spirit guide can be anyone you respect and trust: a therapist, another man who is already on his healing journey, a close friend, or a lover.

The Courageous Act

At some point in his journey the hero is faced with a challenge of enormous proportions. He may have to do battle with a frightening creature or another person. Usually the hero has to use not only his physical strength but other resources, such as feeling, intelligence, intuition, or sensitivity. The hero has to put aside his ego, become humble, and do what is neccessary to complete the task.

You will find many challenges in healing from childhood abuse. You will have to do battle with your inner abuser's tendency to blame yourself for the abuse. Combating low self-esteem is another challenge of the healing process. Learning to get in touch with your feelings may be the greatest challenge of all.

The Return

When the hero returns from his journey there is something different about him. The courageous act has brought about an inner change that others notice immediately. You may even notice the difference yourself, feeling more centered, at peace with yourself or happier with life. You may not feel noticeably different from the way you felt last week, but you may feel radically different than you did six months or a year ago.

Leaving and Returning

Your healing journey will consist of a similar process of leaving a safe and comfortable place, facing and meeting a challenge, and returning with a new attitude or other change. After a while you will venture out again to face new hurdles and overcome new barriers to finding peace of mind. But with each journey you will develop new skills to make the next one easier.

Facing the intense pain of childhood abuse takes courage of heroic proportions. You are a hero for answering the call no matter in what form it came. You are a hero for asking for help and taking deliberate steps in healing your wounds. You are a hero for facing your inner demons and reclaiming your lost self. You are a hero for continuing to struggle with your wounds and make peace with yourself and others.